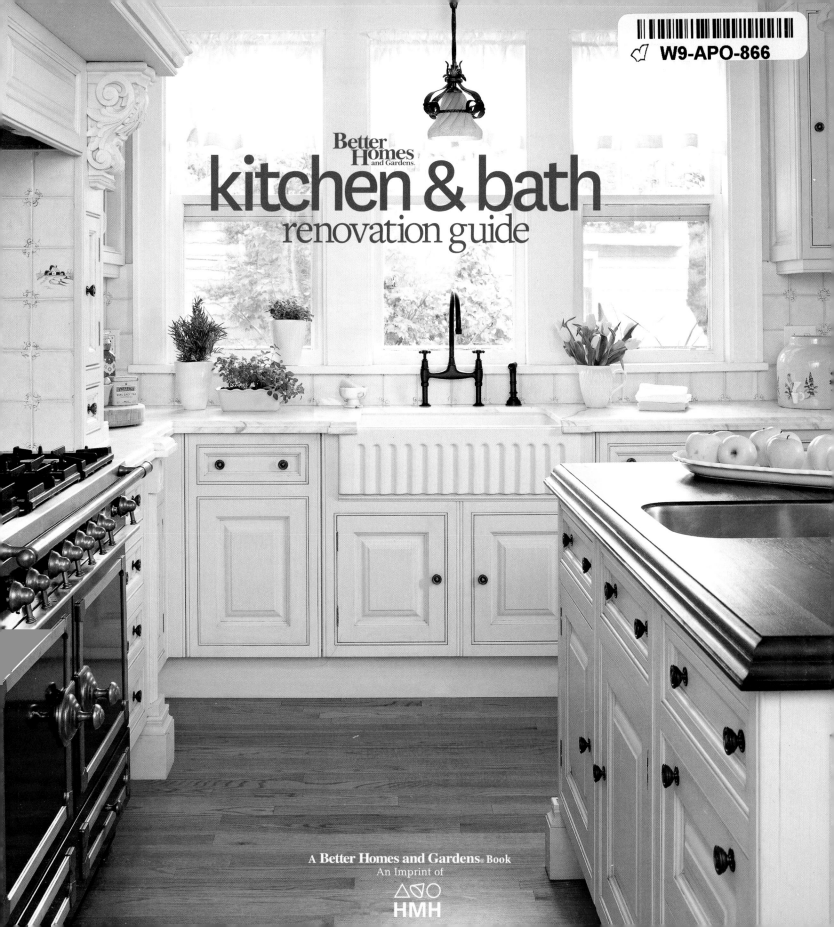

Better Homes and Gardens.

kitchen & bath
renovation guide

A **Better Homes and Gardens** Book
An Imprint of

HMH

Published by:
Houghton Mifflin Harcourt
Boston • New York
www.hmhco.com

For information about permission to reproduce selections from this book, write to Permissions, Houghton Mifflin Harcourt Publishing Company, 215 Park Avenue South, New York, New York 10003.

The publisher and author make no representations or warranties with respect to the accuracy or completeness of the contents of this work and specifically disclaim all warranties, including without limitation warranties of fitness for a particular purpose. No warranty may be created or extended by sales or promotional materials. The advice and strategies contained herein may not be suitable for every situation. This work is sold with the understanding that the publisher is not engaged in rendering legal, accounting, or other professional services. If professional assistance is required, the services of a competent professional person should be sought. Neither the publisher nor the author shall be liable for damages arising here from. The fact that an organization or Website is referred to in this work as a citation and/or a potential source of further information does not mean that the author or the publisher endorses the information the organization or Website may provide or recommendations it may take. Further, readers should be aware that Websites listed in this work may have changed or disappeared between when this work was written and when it is read.

Library of Congress Control Number available from the publisher upon request.
ISBN: 978-0-544-28637-5 (pbk); 978-0-544-28801-0 (ebk)

Printed in the United States of America

DOW 10 9 8 7 6 5 4 3 2 1

NOTE TO THE READERS: Due to differing conditions, tools, and individual skills, Houghton Mifflin Harcourt assumes no responsibility for any damages, injuries suffered, or losses incurred as a result of following the information published in this book. Before beginning any project, review the instructions carefully, and if any doubts or questions remain, consult local experts or authorities. Because codes and regulations vary greatly, you always should check with authorities to ensure that your project complies with all applicable local codes and regulations. Always read and observe all of the safety precautions provided by manufacturers of any tools, equipment, or supplies, and follow all accepted safety procedures.

BETTER HOMES AND GARDENS® MAGAZINE
Gayle Goodson Butler
Executive Vice President, Creative Content Leader
Oma Blaise Ford
Executive Editor
Michael D. Belknap
Creative Director

BETTER HOMES AND GARDENS®
KITCHEN & BATH RENOVATION GUIDE
Contributing Editor: Renee Freemon Mulvihill
Contributing Designer: Gayle Schadendorf
Contributing Copy Editor: Carrie Schmitz
Contributing Writers: Andria Hayday, Debra Steilen
Contributing Illustrator: Michael Burns
Cover Photographer: Paul Dyer
Cover Stylist: Sarah Alba

SPECIAL INTEREST MEDIA
Editorial Director: James D. Blume
Content Director, Home Design: Jill Waage
Deputy Content Director, Home Design: Karman Hotchkiss
Managing Editor: Doug Kouma
Senior Design Director: Gene Rauch
Group Editor: Samantha Hart
Assistant Managing Editor: Jennifer Speer Ramundt
Business Director: Janice Croat

MEREDITH NATIONAL MEDIA GROUP
President: Tom Harty
Director, Operations and Business Development: Doug Olson

MEREDITH CORPORATION
Chairman and Chief Executive Officer: Stephen M. Lacy

HOUGHTON MIFFLIN HARCOURT
Vice President and Publisher: Natalie Chapman
Editorial Director: Cindy Kitchel
Executive Editor, Brands: Anne Ficklen
Associate Editor: Heather Dabah
Managing Editor: Marina Padakis Lowry
Production Editor: Donna Wright
Production Director: Tom Hyland

Welcome

Whether you're dreaming of adding a marble-topped island to your cramped kitchen or transforming your dated bath into a soothing, spa-like retreat, we've filled this book with tips and advice to help you jump-start your renovation project—and keep it on track. Take a look at inspiring before-and-after makeovers, and start planning your new room! You'll find helpful hints about hiring design professionals and crafting a floor plan that works for you, as well as decorating and storage tips that can help give your space fresh style and function. And don't forget to take a look at our shopping guide for advice about all the products you'll need to create your dream space.

contents

before & after

These inspiring kitchen and bath transformations showcase how eye-catching design elements and efficient layouts can bring fresh and functional style to any room.

quick & easy makeover

This kitchen gained a fresh perspective with painted cabinets, new appliances and fixtures, and pretty shelving.

before

The layout in this galley kitchen worked well—the space just needed some freshening up to make it feel open and inviting. To save money, designer Donna Talley retained some of the existing cabinetry—updating the look with a coat of sage green paint—and replaced some of the upper cabinets with decorative shelving to lighten the look in the small prep zone. New stainless-steel appliances offer modern convenience, and new light fixtures and window treatments add sophisticated style. To unite the cooking zone with the adjacent step-down dining area, the team extended the kitchen countertop to create a convenient dining peninsula that makes smart use of existing space.

OPEN SHELVING, *far right,* replaces a chunky soffit and upper cabinets to create the illusion of more space. Marble-look laminate countertops offer high-end style at a budget-friendly price.

THE CLEANUP ZONE, *right,* gets a new look with a pretty valance and a bronze pendant light. A new, deeper sink makes washing large pots easy.

quick & easy makeover

A NEW RANGE and hood combine modern convenience and style. Existing cabinets were painted for a fresh look, while new subway tile on the backsplash adds vintage appeal.

before

STYLISH DINING, *left,* becomes part of the kitchen thanks to an extended countertop; it creates a space-savvy dining bar and unites the kitchen work area and adjacent step-down dining space. Barstool seating elevates diners, allowing them to easily converse with the cook.

AN EFFICIENT PANTRY, *below, far left,* features two tall doors instead of the original four doors, offering a sleeker look and easier access to the pantry's contents.

PULLOUT SHELVES, *below left,* were added to existing cabinets to keep pots and pans organized and within easy reach of the cook.

A REPURPOSED HUTCH, *below,* was painted and topped with a new countertop to create a handy bar and serving area. Linens are stored in the hutch's wide drawer, while new pullout shelves corral additional bar items below.

small-kitchen upgrade

Charming cottage details and smart layout tweaks give this once-dated galley kitchen additional work space and a more inviting look—without toppling walls or breaking the bank.

before

What can you do with a string of weekends, about $5,500, and a frumpy 9×16-foot kitchen with virtually no counter space and even less character? Quite a lot, if you're designer Tracy Wills, who transformed her 1970s kitchen with more moxie than money. Tracy and her husband, Bill, stripped the kitchen bare one section at a time, reworking each area in turn as they found time. To save thousands, they bought unfinished, off-the-shelf cabinets in oak, then dressed them up using moldings and other cleverly applied millwork. Painted white and contrasted with dark wood countertops, the budget-friendly cabinets look custom and exude cottage charm.

The revamped layout is equally smart— showing off improved function within the room's original footprint. Before the remodel, the refrigerator crowded the cooktop, and a wall oven consumed precious counter space. Replacing the cooktop and wall oven with a slide-in range added countertop work space, and a new counter-depth refrigerator (positioned where the wall oven used to be) preserves floor space. Across the aisle, a new apron-front sink adds vintage charm, and open shelves give the small kitchen an airy look.

At the far end of the room, a tiny breakfast area was once a crowded tangle of chairs. But now a space-saving window seat, a cottage-style pedestal table, and two storage-packed pantries create a cozy dining space with a streamlined, built-in look.

PAINTED WALLPAPER on the backsplash, *above right,* mimics the look of pressed tin at a budget-friendly price.

STAIR BALUSTERS were cut in half and set atop curtain-rod finials, *right,* to elegantly frame the sink cabinet.

A SLIDE-IN RANGE, *opposite,* replaced a cooktop and wall oven, adding counter space and making a new home for the refrigerator.

small-kitchen upgrade

before

OPEN SHELVES replace bulky cabinets above a new farmhouse sink, *left*, visually opening up the narrow room. Wood counters add warmth and contrast, complementing a bronze faucet. Stenciling enlivens the whitewashed oak floor and adds custom detail.

A WINDOW SEAT tucks in between tall pantry cabinets, *opposite*, utilizing a blank wall in the breakfast area. The seat's top opens to offer storage for large stockpots and other bulky items. A pendant light was made from a wire flower-basket, while an old lamp base became the table's pedestal.

before

gathering space

A new island and dining table, paired with old-world decorating details, upgrade a lackluster kitchen into a warm and welcoming space for entertaining.

before

A NEW OPEN LAYOUT shows off a generous island with a custom table, *right,* that can be pulled away from the island to seat up to 12 dinner guests.

Sometimes a kitchen doesn't have to grow any larger to ease entertaining—it just needs to be a little more grown-up. Designers Debbie Nassetta and Ginger Brewsaugh opened up this kitchen and merged it with an adjacent family room through careful subtraction. Space-eating walk-in pantry and wall ovens? Gone. Banquette in the bay window? Gone. Divisive peninsula with a snack bar? Gone and good riddance.

The original builder-grade kitchen seemed adequate in the 1980s, but as years passed, the plan felt increasingly crowded and choppy. The cooktop was squeezed into an undersize island, and the banquette was too small and mundane for entertaining.

The new plan puts a large, pewter-topped island with a generously sized prep sink directly opposite a pro-grade range and custom hood, while the bay window now showcases a cleanup zone. The kitchen's most flexible feature is a custom table with a double pedestal that can be pulled away from the island to expand seating.

With its easy circulation and updated old-world style, this kitchen is ideal for hosting extended family and friends. And as grown children return with children of their own, they'll still feel right at home.

gathering space

before

A CUSTOM HUTCH, *right*, conceals the refrigerator and pantry. Beveled mirrors hide auxiliary dishware storage and reflect a pretty view.

SMART STORAGE near the range, *below,* includes a pullout for hanging cooking tools, dish towels, or potholders. A second pullout holds spices.

THE ISLAND'S PEWTER TOP, *below right*, scratches easily, but its evolving patina is part of its charm. The fireclay prep sink, situated across from the range, anchors an efficient prep zone.

A MICROWAVE DRAWER tucks discreetly into the island, *below, far right*, maintaining the kitchen's emphasis on furnishings rather than appliances.

A PRO-STYLE RANGE and custom hood serve as a focal point on the kitchen's far wall. Granite countertops, limestone and travertine backsplash tiles, and travertine flooring enhance the room's sophisticated look.

Warm & Welcoming
GIVE YOUR KITCHEN LIVING ROOM STYLE WITH THESE TIPS.

- Conceal appliances; wherever possible, treat them like furniture. Disguise the refrigerator as a hutch, for example, or face appliances with cabinet panels. Tuck small appliances behind cabinet doors.
- Limit traditional wall-hung cabinets, and instead make the most of undercounter storage to help the kitchen blend with adjacent living areas.
- Separate seated guests from dirty dishes. Place the cleanup zone away from gathering areas, and choose an extra-large, deep sink to help hide the mess. Consider adding an auxiliary dishwasher.
- Arrange the room so that guests can help themselves to a beverage without getting in the cook's way. Incorporate wide aisles to eliminate bottlenecks.
- Include layers of flexible lighting to illuminate prep areas and set the mood for entertaining.

everyday luxury

Merging three small rooms into one created a spacious and inviting cooking zone that's as much a family hangout space as an efficient work area.

before

GLASS-FRONT CABINETS soar to a coffered ceiling in this fresh, airy kitchen, *right,* amplifying storage space. Beveled subway tiles and marble counters gracefully partner with clean-lined cabinets with subtle beaded detail. Dark oak floors ground the cooking space and lend traditional charm.

Like many old houses, this 1917 Italianate beauty in San Francisco began with a warren of rooms at the back, including a tiny kitchen, a walk-through butler's pantry, and an isolated breakfast room. To one side of the kitchen, a closed-in stairwell faced the neighbor's garden, keeping the view all to itself.

Prior residents had updated the decor but left the divisive floor plan, so architect David S. Gast merged all three rooms into a single glorious space with soaring walls and a coffered ceiling. The old stairwell is gone, replaced by a window-wrapped banquette that floods the kitchen with light.

At the heart of the new layout, a marble-topped island divides the room into two zones: one for prep work and cooking, and the other for cleanup. The island's prep sink is just a step away from the cooktop and wall ovens.

The room's classic white-painted millwork befits the house, but its fresh, airy look suits the young family who lives here. The cabinetry is clean-lined, with understated beaded detail and square, chunky feet. Hot-pink throw pillows enliven the banquette, where the striped upholstery is fashionable, easy-care outdoor fabric.

From cookie-making to crafts to grown-up gatherings, the room handles all kinds of tasks with ease. Before, the kitchen was a trap for one lonely cook. Now it's the most welcoming room in the house.

everyday luxury

before

TWO DISHWASHERS
flank the cleanup
zone's apron-front sink,
opposite. The sink area
was moved from an
adjacent wall that was
taken out when several
rooms were combined.

A BANQUETTE, *left,*
features stain- and
fade-resistant outdoor
upholstery, completing
a plush, family-friendly
hangout. The table's
gently distressed
surface helps scratches
blend in.

everyday luxury

A HARDWORKING ISLAND holds the microwave, pullout baskets for produce, and abundant storage, *below*. The prep sink's off-center location maximizes counter space in the work zone.

TALL STORAGE surrounds the refrigerator and a built-in steam oven, *right*. Doors above the oven conceal a television, and cabinets keep canned goods, cookie sheets, and crafts supplies organized.

before

A SIX-BURNER COOKTOP, *left,* is a pivot-turn from the island's prep sink, completing a classic work triangle with the refrigerator (far right, not shown). Double wall ovens make it easy to cook for a crowd.

powder room drama

Classic European details and a mix of old and new materials inject fresh style into this narrow bath. Budget-friendly finds helped the designer get a custom look for less.

before

Traditional but fresh, this powder room in an 1860s home once had a single virtue: Its toilet was discreetly located to the side, so it wasn't visible from the hall. If only the original vanity had been a worthy focal point. Set directly opposite the entry, it was a cobbled-together piece that interfered with the door-swing in the narrow 3×8-foot plan.

Unfazed, designer Donna Talley began sleuthing for a sink replacement that would fit her bath's tight footprint—and her equally tight budget. Her find: a $150 antique-reproduction table with a painted finish, X braces on the sides and back, and just enough room for a small sink. The price was sweet, but the style clinched the deal. "I've long admired the Belgian aesthetic—a neutral color palette and clean lines mixed with weathered furnishings and a blend of old and new elements—so I decided to carry this look into the powder room," Donna says.

The vanity still needed a little "wow," so Donna boosted its style with an ornate oval mirror, which contrasts with the table's earthy finish. For added polish, she splurged on a wall-hung faucet in chrome, offsetting its cost with a petite white vessel sink found online.

To complete the room, Donna painted the walls creamy beige and repainted the wood floor (originally green) using a darker shade of cream. Then she wrapped the toilet area with a chic gallery of black-and-white photos. Pleasing from every angle, the bath now extends a fitting welcome to guests.

AN EYE-CATCHING GALLERY of black-and-white photographs, *above,* adds interest to the toilet area. The designer used an online service to reproduce her own photos and chose white matting and black frames for a cohesive look.

THE VANITY, *left,* was created from an antique-reproduction table; its open base helps to visually expand the room. The oval mirror—a thrift-shop find—was updated with metallic paint.

BRUSHED NICKEL pairs with faux alabaster in the transitional-style ceiling light, *top.*

CROSS HANDLES add charm to the wall-hung faucet, *above.* With a price tag of $240, it was the most expensive purchase for the bath; the chrome finish adds sparkle and contrasts with the wood vanity and textural accessories.

stylish small bath

A light and lively color scheme and careful layout tweaks that make better use of headroom transformed a cramped bath into an inviting and airy retreat.

before

A SKYLIGHT brings in natural light above the claw-foot tub, *right,* which sits in its original location. A built-in niche beside the tub offers handy recessed storage.

WORTH THE SPLURGE, the shower, *opposite,* features a $2,800 custom glass enclosure. White subway tile dresses the shower's other walls. Centered over the room, a drum-style light fixture makes a modern statement.

"My dirty little secret." That's how interior designer Julie Fergus used to describe this bath in her Cape Cod–style home. Tucked under the steep roof, the room originally held an ugly plywood vanity, dingy-looking carpet, and no shower—just an old claw-foot tub.

The sloped ceiling presented some layout challenges, but Julie knew she could make things better. Originally, the vanity sat below the ridgeline like a lonely centerpiece. Seizing the prime headroom, Julie gave this spot to a luxurious new shower instead, adding a wall to anchor the showerhead. She also wrapped knee walls around the tub. The new walls subtract a little floor space, but they instill visual order. Plus, they hide plumbing and provide staging for built-in storage cubbies.

Julie converted a pretty sideboard into a vanity and tucked it below the angled ceiling. The vintage piece fit perfectly—as soon as Julie shortened the legs a bit. A low-profile vessel sink sits off-center so no one has to duck while grooming.

For the walls and ceiling, Julie chose pine planks painted cottage white. "I wanted an antique look that you can't get with Sheetrock," Julie says. Extra-wide planks cover the floor, where they are painted a bright apple green. Julie extended the same green to the exterior of the tub, which nestles beneath a dreamy new skylight.

The results were so enticing that Julie and her husband decided to claim an adjacent bedroom and make this bath their master. It's no longer a "dirty little secret"—instead, it's more like a secret getaway.

Bright apple-green paint on the floor gives the bath a playful, cottage appeal.

Solutions for Small Spaces

USE THESE TIPS TO MAKE YOUR SMALL BATH LIVE LARGE.

- Tuck storage into the walls. Knee walls accommodate deep cubbies, but even a 3½-inch-deep shelf recessed between wall studs can hold toiletries. With 5–6 inches of depth, you can stash toilet paper or include an outlet for an electric toothbrush or razor.
- Stretch sight lines. Choose a vanity that lets you see below it—a pedestal sink, a floating vanity, or a leggy console, for example. Wrap the shower with a frameless glass enclosure, and make generous use of mirrors where possible.
- Make the most of available headroom in an attic or dormered space. A station that's used while seated—the toilet, a soaking tub, a bench—can tuck into an area of decreasing height.
- Claim a view. Add a skylight above a tub or a window in the shower (just keep it above shoulder height and add waterproofing).

stylish small bath

A TALL, SLIM FAUCET, *above*, sits directly on the rim of the sink, saving counter space. Less costly than a wall-hung faucet, the single-lever design combines ease of use with vintage charm.

A STORAGE CUBBY for towels and spare toilet paper tucks into a planked knee wall behind the toilet, *right*. Pulled away from the cold exterior, plumbing lines in the new knee wall are protected from winter freeze-ups.

A REPURPOSED SIDEBOARD became the perfect vanity, *opposite*, once its legs were trimmed and its top was sealed with a water-resistant finish. A retractable mirror eases makeup application. An existing dormer window (glimpsed left) balances the skylight across the room.

vintage charmer

Old-fashioned details celebrate the past and elevate this small bungalow bath to new heights. Creative, DIY-friendly solutions add designer looks at an affordable price.

before

The hexagonal mosaic floor tile in this 1920s bungalow is definitely the "right stuff." An original feature, it's still in great shape, and its blue-and-white pattern will always feel classic. Ditto for the crystal knobs on the built-in linen cupboard and the Arts-and-Crafts trim that stretches through the house.

If only the rest of this bath had held up so well. After 30 years in residence, the owners were faced with a leaky toilet, a stained sink, and outdated decor.

Taking cues from the floor, they revived the bath using a blue-and-white palette. Noting the indent from an old chair rail, they added white beaded-board paneling on the lower walls. Next they installed a new white toilet and sink and added reeded-glass doors to the linen cabinet to visually expand the room.

With so much white as a foundation, the owners knew they could be a little daring on the upper walls. Bright blue paint could have worked, but it seemed too boring, too matchy-matchy. Instead, they chose a dark blue-and-gray wallpaper with a sophisticated pattern. Finishing touches include an oval medicine cabinet (framed in white, of course), new vintage-style lighting, and bright chrome accessories with old-fashioned charm. The result is a polished, pulled-together look that promises to stand the test of time.

A CURVED ROD for the shower curtain, *right*, expands a standard tub and shower. Positioned close to the ceiling, it also makes the 4×8-foot room feel taller.

MIRRORED HOOKS with crystal accents, *far right*, hold his-and-her robes and coordinate with the bath's original crystal hardware.

WHITE BEADED BOARD suits this bath's classic cottage style, including the original hexagonal tile floor, *left*. A pedestal sink keeps the narrow space from feeling crowded.

vintage charmer

REEDED-GLASS insets added to the linen cupboard's existing doors, *above*, subtly echo the lines of the room's beaded board.

GROSGRAIN RIBBON offers an inexpensive way to give a plain shower curtain and Roman window shade, *above right*, a designer look.

AN EMBROIDERED MONOGRAM added to the shower curtain, *right*, personalizes the space and repeats the eye-catching curves found in the wallpaper's gray swirls.

VINTAGE LIGHTING, *far right,* pairs curved chrome arms with frosted glass shades for a timeless look.

A BROAD RIM and a squared-off, extra-wide bowl enhance the new pedestal sink. A glass shelf and recessed medicine cabinet amplify storage.

spa-like retreat

This calming sanctuary shows off luxurious amenities and cutting-edge design, thanks to an expanded layout and a mix of sculptural forms and textural materials.

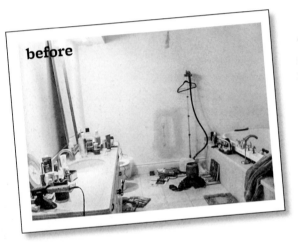

before

This bath offers a host of luxuries: an enticing soaking tub, a gentle rain-style shower, muscle-pummeling water jets, and a steam shower for two. Designed to bring the spa experience home, the bath offers a place to unwind and unplug, cocooned by soft music, sensual lighting, and soul-soothing warmth.

In order to incorporate a long list of amenities into an already-crowded space, designer Nathalie Tremblay began by toppling a wall to annex a closet. Then she reworked the entire layout, floating a freestanding tub near the middle of the room and stretching a wall of glass behind it to define a shower alcove. The result is a fabulous walk-through shower with doors on either side of the tub, complete with a dry zone for toweling off.

Previously, a bulky platform tub sat beneath the room's only windows. Now the same box-bay holds a dressing bench, cleverly integrated with a floating vanity on the adjacent wall. Once awkwardly exposed, the toilet has been relocated to a private compartment complete with a TV and a petite wall-hung sink.

Clean-lined and calm, the decor is a study in contrasts. Silky-smooth white fixtures are countered by a textural slate wall, and built-ins are painted charcoal gray and gloss white. White marble stretches to the ceiling on the vanity wall, continuing across the floor and into the shower. Painted soft gray, the remaining walls play off veining in the marble and create visual harmony.

THE TUB FILLER complements the tub's modern form, *right*. Its handheld shower extends the full length of the tub, enhancing convenience when bathing or cleaning.

A SCULPTURAL TUB, *opposite*, moves into a new position of prominence at the center of the room. It's set off by a backdrop of stacked-slate tile. A wall-hung television and towel warmer add everyday luxury.

spa-like retreat

QUARTZ-SURFACING tops the floating vanity, *above*, where a white trough-style sink serves two faucets. A stone shelf above the sink continues into the private toilet compartment (far left).

SLEEK WALL-HUNG FAUCETS, *left*, feature rectilinear backplates that mimic the shape of the sink and the marble backsplash tiles, which are installed in a staggered, running bond pattern.

THE FLOATING VANITY with open storage for towels, *opposite*, interlocks with a window seat. The built-ins are made of riftsawn oak and paired with an open shelf painted gloss white. Glass drawer pulls complement the cabinetry's sleek look.

The Spa Experience

KEEP THESE DESIGN CONSIDERATIONS IN MIND WHEN ADDING PAMPERING AMENITIES TO YOUR BATH.

- Plumbing lines. Be sure your plumbing and water heater can handle your bath's new features. Multiple showerheads require adequate supply lines and water pressure to function properly.
- Water consumption. Consider installing low-flow faucets and showerheads (look for models with the WaterSense label) and high-efficiency or dual-flush toilets to reduce water usage.
- Overall comfort. Consider including radiant heat under tile or stone floors, a heated shower bench, or towel warmers.
- Uncluttered style. A spa environment is clean-lined, airy, and free of visual clutter, so steer clear of busy patterns, ultra-bright colors, and shelves filled with collectibles.
- Smart technology. Consider adding a built-in sound system or a shower system that includes music and mood lighting. Some shower systems allow you to save preferences for water temperature and massage settings.

spa-like retreat

A DRY ZONE in the glass-enclosed steam shower, *left*, includes shelving for towels and artful displays.

A FLAT-PANEL television is mounted on the stacked-slate wall near the tub, *above right*. The slate wall adds a masculine touch to the bath. Another television (not shown) hangs in the private toilet compartment.

SWAROVSKI CRYSTAL floor lights sparkle beside the tub, *right*. Trapezoidal tiles bring a contemporary look to the marble floor. Heated coils under the tile warm the floor at specific times of day via a built-in timer.

A NICHE built into the shower, *below right*, keeps shampoos within easy reach but preserves the bath's uncluttered look.

"Edgy and modern, this bath also contains the five age-old elements of feng shui: earth, wood, fire, metal, and water." —*Designer* Nathalie Tremblay

before

THE NEW SHOWER stretches across one side of the bath, *left*, bearing little resemblance to the former bath's cramped shower stall. The new steam shower features two rain-style showerheads, a handheld shower spray, and operable glass transoms up top that allow steam to escape when desired.

architectural elegance

Painted wood paneling echoes the rhythm of this bath's luxurious marble tile, creating an elegant retreat that finally complements the character of this historical home.

before

Although the 1920s house had plenty of vintage charm, the dated upstairs bath left a lot to be desired. Serviceable but small, it lacked the modern amenities that would make it a luxurious retreat. But a smart addition at the back of the house created space for a new, generously sized bath that shows off stately stone and charming architectural paneling.

Marble surfaces create the bath's elegant foundation. Large white and gray marble tiles enhance the floor (including the shower), while a pinkish-beige marble adds soft color to the shower walls.

Against this stone, ordinary drywall seemed jarringly lightweight and mundane, so designer Christine Garrett dressed the remaining walls with a grid of wood paneling, sizing the panels to echo the 12-inch wall tile. Painted a rich, creamy hue with pink and gray undertones, the woodwork blends smoothly with both types of marble, giving the bath a sophisticated, pulled-together look and a heightened architectural presence.

The bathroom's pale decor amplifies natural light, and its silvery fixtures heighten the glamour—as does the curvy dressing table that sits between two rectangular sinks. The soaking tub and generous walk-in shower, meanwhile, provide the modern comforts the homeowners desired.

HAMMERED NICKEL adds glamour to the sink, *right,* in one of the bath's marble vanities. Vintage-style faucets feature cross handles with porcelain accents.

CURVED LEGS, *far right,* were inspired by Art Deco designs.

CONSOLE SINKS, *opposite,* visually expand the room. Stylish sconces echo the paneling's vertical lines.

Selecting Stone

CONSIDER STYLE AND DURABILITY WHEN CHOOSING STONE FOR YOUR BATHROOM.

- Weigh aesthetics. Granite offers versatility with its range of colors and patterns, while marble provides a sophisticated look with its distinctive veining. Limestone shows off a natural, earthy appearance, while onyx can make a bold, dramatic statement.

- Consider maintenance. Virtually all stone needs to be sealed regularly, but nonporous stones such as granite tend to be more durable. Softer, more porous stones, such as marble, limestone, and travertine, require regular sealing and cleaning with a neutral-pH formula to avoid staining and pitting.

- Think about safety. Grout lines increase traction, so a stone-mosaic floor is a good choice for showers. If you prefer large-format tile or a stone slab, specify a well-honed finish so it's less slippery. Consider adding a slip-proof rug or teak mat outside the shower or tub to prevent accidents.

architectural elegance

"I used wood paneling to make the bathroom look less like a hotel and more like part of an older home."
—*Designer* Christine Garrett

A CENTRAL AISLE divides the bath, *opposite*, positioning the walk-in shower and soaking tub directly across from the vanities. A German silver chair adds an unexpected focal point opposite the room's entry.

THE SHOWER, *above*, features a curbless design and an inset drain that allows the shower floor to be flush with the bathroom floor. A window in the shower enhances natural light, while a freestanding marble bench and built-in storage niche pair style and convenience.

A DRESSING TABLE, *right*, separates the dual console sinks. Painted-glass shutters enhance privacy without introducing a slat pattern that would conflict with the room's focal-point paneling.

getting started

Careful consideration and planning are key factors in any successful renovation project. Here's what you need to know before you start work on your kitchen or bath.

assessing your needs

As you start to design your new room, take time to consider the benefits and limitations of your current space—so you can design a kitchen or bath that really works for you.

Can't wait to rip out that dated vinyl floor or get rid of that ugly vanity? Although it's tempting to start your kitchen or bath overhaul right away, it's important to take time to consider how you use the space—and how you would like to be able to use it. Thinking carefully about the big picture helps ensure you don't end up with beautiful new cabinets but a kitchen work zone that still feels cramped and uninviting. Here are a few things to consider as you begin to plan your updated kitchen or bathroom.

Take stock of available space.

Before you redesign your kitchen or bath, consider whether the existing space meets your needs. Do you have enough countertop space in the kitchen work zone, for example? Do you have enough room for your family to hang out in the kitchen, or do you long for more storage space? Is your existing bath large enough for a luxurious shower for two, or will you need to find extra space in order to add spa-like amenities? Take time to think about how you want to use your space and which features are most important to you.

Consider traffic flow.

If you're redesigning your kitchen, be sure to think about how cooks and guests use the room. If you find that guests often get in the cook's way, you may want to change the floor plan to reroute traffic around the central cooking area. If you have more than one cook in your family, you'll want to create a kitchen with multiple work zones. Similarly,

in the bath, you may need wider aisles or a dual vanity to accommodate two users during the morning rush hour. Just as importantly, consider how the kitchen or bath connects to adjoining rooms. Would you like to open the kitchen to an adjacent living area or outdoor dining space? Does your bathing area flow seamlessly into the master bedroom and closet? Or would you prefer the bathroom to feel a little more secluded?

Think about accessibility.

If you're hoping to stay in your home as you age, you'll want to include features in your kitchen or bath that will improve safety and ensure easy access to all amenities. Or if you are just starting a family, you'll want to think about including child-friendly storage or a microwave drawer that can be easily used by kids. Smart planning can ensure accessible features are both stylish and functional.

Improve efficiency.

As you get ready to remodel your kitchen or bath, look for ways you can also improve your home's energy efficiency. New windows and appliances can help you decrease home energy costs, so now might be a good time to replace them. Look for Energy Star-certified models that meet energy-efficiency standards set by the Environmental Protection Agency. If you'll be renovating your bath, replace old fixtures with high-efficiency or dual-flush toilets or low-flow showerheads. Installing Energy Star LED light fixtures and dimmer switches can be other good ways to go green.

DIY TIP
Hoping to enlarge your island or change the placement for your tub? Mark the new outline on the floor with tape and live with it for a few days—to make sure it works as well as you envision.

setting a budget

Before you start construction work or hire any professionals, sit down and establish a budget for your home improvement project—then stick to it.

Figuring out a budget for your kitchen or bath project might not be as much fun as selecting fixtures and paint colors, but it's just as important—if not more so. To begin, think about how long you plan to stay in your home. If you plan to move within a few years, investigate home prices in your area and be careful to keep your budget in line with the average home price. On the other hand, if you plan to remain in your home for many years, spend as much as you can comfortably afford to create your dream home.

To determine what you are comfortable spending on your renovation, make a list of all your debts and figure out your monthly gross income. From here, you can determine the maximum monthly payment you can afford to spend on remodeling costs. Talk to a lender about financing options, if necessary.

Remember that building and remodeling almost always end up costing more than expected. Experts recommend adding a cushion of at least 10 percent to your overall budget to account for surprises along the way.

10 WAYS TO KEEP YOUR BUDGET ON TRACK

1. HAVE FIRM GOALS AND STICK TO THEM.
It can be easy to get distracted by all the glamorous products on the market, but they can quickly derail your budget. Focus on your main goals and choose products accordingly, opting for a few splurges along the way.

2. BRING IN THE PROS.
Architects and designers increase initial costs, but they can save you money in the long run by helping you avoid design pitfalls and suggesting ways to save money on design and materials.

3. KEEP IT SIMPLE.
If you're remodeling, try to keep load-bearing walls where they are and avoid rerouting plumbing and electrical lines. Varied rooflines, curved walls, arches, and bump-outs all enhance the character of a kitchen, but they also bump up the cost.

4. CHECK CONTRACTOR REFERENCES.
If you'll be hiring a contractor to help you with construction work, be sure to ask references about the contractor's communication skills, follow-through, and adherence to deadlines. If the contractor regularly misses deadlines and communicates poorly, you'll likely end up with inflated bills and extra stress.

5. ORDER MATERIALS IN ADVANCE.
Some custom items, such as windows and cabinetry, take several weeks to arrive. Keep your job's progress on track by having materials on hand before any work begins.

6. STICK WITH WHAT'S IN STOCK.
Custom windows, cabinetry, and other items can drive up project costs. Look for standard and semicustom goods, which are often available in a range of styles and price levels to help keep your budget on track.

7. LOOK FOR DEALS.
Shop your local home center for clearance items, end-of-season sales, discontinued products, and floor models. You can also find great deals online—just be sure you know what you're buying.

8. KEEP CHANGES TO A MINIMUM.
Some changes are inevitable, but making alterations to renovation plans midway through the project is a quick way to ruin your budget. If you make changes after plumbing, electrical, and drywall work is done, you'll likely have to tear out finished work and start over—and pay for the work twice.

9. MAKE SMART TRADE-OFFS.
If you're forced to make difficult choices to keep your budget on track, sacrifice items that can easily be retrofitted later. Choose less-expensive lights, faucets, window treatments, and door and cabinet hardware, and put your money toward cabinets, countertops, and other labor-intensive items.

10. HELP OUT WITH THE WORK.
Even inexperienced do-it-yourselfers can remove old cabinets, fixtures, and other items that will be replaced. And once the major construction work is done, you can step back in and help with painting, installing faucets and lights, and other finishing details.

hiring professionals

Take time to consider the details of how the construction work will be handled—from what projects you'll do yourself, what tasks are best left to the pros, and what needs to be done when.

Can you handle the work yourself, or do you need to hire professionals to help with design or installation? If you're planning a complete kitchen or bath overhaul, you'll likely benefit from design help, even if you are willing to do the construction work yourself. To find a qualified professional, ask family and friends for references, or visit a local home show or neighborhood home tour and talk with representatives there. Plan to meet with several design professionals or contractors, ask to see examples of prior work, and take time to speak with references. Choose a firm that has worked on projects that are similar to your own in size and scope.

Several types of design professionals are available to help you with a kitchen or bath renovation project, so it can sometimes be difficult to know who to hire. Here's a brief description of various professionals in the remodeling and building industry—and a look at how they can help you create the kitchen or bath of your dreams.

Architect

If you're planning a major remodeling project or addition, an architect can help you determine the overall design and create construction drawings that are required for obtaining building permits. These professionals help you maintain the structural integrity of your home and ensure that an addition complements the scale and design of your existing house. Architects have formal education and experience and are licensed by the state. In addition to designing the space, some architects are also willing to help manage the remodeling project. Find an architect near you by visiting the American Institute of Architects website: *aia.org.*

Kitchen or bath designer

These professionals can also help you create the construction drawings necessary for your project. They can be an excellent choice if you'll be significantly changing your kitchen or bathroom layout—but not altering the design of your whole house. Certified kitchen and bath designers specialize in kitchen or bath design, so they are very familiar with the design guidelines and requirements for cooking and bathing spaces. They must meet specified educational requirements and follow a professional code of ethics outlined by the National Kitchen & Bath Association (NKBA). To find a professional near you, look at the list of designers on the NKBA website: *nkba.org.*

General contractor

A contractor manages the construction work required to create your dream kitchen or bath. They might do the work themselves or, more likely, hire subcontractors to handle part or all of the project. If you are planning a small remodeling project and are not rearranging rooms, you might not need professional design services and can work directly with an experienced contractor.

DIY TIP
If you'll be hiring subcontractors yourself, find potential candidates by asking at plumbing supply stores or tile shops—or get tips from other subcontractors. Be sure to get two or three bids for each job, and check references carefully.

Make sure any bids you obtain from contractors clearly spell out all the details of the project, including the scope of the work, specific materials that will be used, and warranties. Beware of extremely low bids—they may be tempting but often result in added costs later and/or shoddy workmanship and low-quality materials.

Design-build contractor

A design-build firm can oversee both the design and construction services, thus simplifying the remodeling process and allowing you to work with the same person throughout the project. Some firms have architects on staff, while others use certified designers, so be sure to ask about the staff's credentials. Because a design-build firm oversees your project from initial design through completion, the professionals can suggest architectural alterations with your budget in mind—helping to ensure your overall remodeling costs don't get out of hand as your project is under way.

Interior designer

These design professionals can help you ensure your finished space is both comfortable and functional. They can help you select furniture, fabric, lighting fixtures, wall coverings, and window treatments. They can also help address space planning, organization and storage, and safety issues. If you don't have enough money in your budget to hire an interior designer to help throughout your renovation project, you may be able to hire one for an initial consultation. For a flat fee or an hourly rate, many are willing to meet with you and offer general advice and design ideas. To find an interior designer in your area, visit the American Society of Interior Designers website: *asid.org.*

What to Ask When Interviewing a Professional

YOU CAN SIGNIFICANTLY INCREASE YOUR CHANCES OF A SUCCESSFUL REMODELING PROJECT BY CAREFULLY INTERVIEWING PROFESSIONALS AND CHECKING REFERENCES. HERE ARE A FEW QUESTIONS SUGGESTED BY THE NATIONAL ASSOCIATION OF THE REMODELING INDUSTRY TO HELP YOU FIND THE RIGHT PERSON FOR YOUR JOB.

How long have you been in business?
Look for a contractor or design firm with an established business history in your area, and ask contractors for current copies of their license and their certification of insurance.

Does your firm carry workers' compensation and liability insurance?
Most states require contractors to carry workers' compensation, property damage, and personal liability insurance. Verify that the contractor's insurance coverage meets your state's minimum requirements.

How is your firm organized?
Find out if the company has employees or hires subcontractors. Will there be a project supervisor or lead carpenter to oversee your project?

How many similar projects have you completed in the past 12 months?
Look for designers and/or contractors who are familiar with your desired design style and/or project type.

What percentage of your business is repeat or referral business?
This answer can give you a helpful hint about customer satisfaction.

May I have a list of references?
Ask for a minimum of three references, and specifically inquire about projects that are similar to your own. You can also see if the designer or contractor can arrange visits to finished job sites.

signing a contract

Whether you're hiring an architect, a designer, a general contractor, or subcontractors, it's best to have everyone sign on the dotted line before work begins.

DIY TIP
If you'll be acting as your own general contractor, don't forget to acquire the necessary building permits before starting construction work. Contact your local permitting office to find out about codes in your area.

If you'll be hiring a contractor to help you with your kitchen or bath project, be sure to carefully examine the contract. This is the document that outlines the scope of the project and ensures everyone is in agreement about who will handle what. Consider having a legal professional review the document before you sign it, and make sure you understand everything that is included in (and excluded from) the document.

Key components
Make sure the contract contains the following:
- The contractor's name, address, phone number, and license number (if applicable)

- Details about materials for the project, including size, color, model, and brand name for all products

- A clear description of what the contractor will and will not do, such as protect personal property at the job site, daily cleanup, and cleanup upon completion of the job

- Approximate start date and completion dates for the project

- The total price, payment schedule, and any cancellation penalties

- A full or limited warranty covering materials and workmanship for a minimum of one year (this should include the name and address of the party who will honor the warranty—the contractor, distributor, or manufacturer)

- A binding arbitration clause that may allow you to resolve disputes without costly litigation if a disagreement occurs

Change orders
Most remodeling and building projects will require a change order at some point—a written document to alter, change, or remove items found in the original contract. You may change your mind about a specific product or design, the contractor may suggest changing some aspect of the design, or extra work may be needed to fix an unexpected discovery, such as termite damage. Make sure that any change to the contract is done in writing and signed by all parties before any work is completed. Before signing, ask about the price of the changes and the added work time they may require. Be sure to keep a copy for your records.

The finish line
Before making your final payment, plan to walk through your finished kitchen or bath with your contractor, architect, or designer, and discuss anything that still needs to be changed or completed. Often firms will use a punch list, which is a written document that lists all the corrections or changes that must be completed to the homeowner's satisfaction. It's also a good idea to request signed lien releases from any major suppliers or subcontractors—this protects you financially if your general contractor does not pay final bills for materials and supplies..

surviving a remodel

Any kitchen or bath remodel takes time and requires patience and smart planning. Here's how to handle the mess and upheaval that goes along with a remodeling project.

Living in a house while major construction work is being done is never easy—plan for at least a few rough weeks. It's easy to get overwhelmed by all the inconvenience, dust, and noise, but you can eliminate some of the stress by planning ahead. Follow these tips to ease the headaches and frustration that often come with a remodeling project.

Prepare mentally and emotionally.
Even if you hate the way your kitchen or bath looks now, you might be unprepared for the emotional upheaval that comes with tearing a room to the bare studs. It doesn't look pretty—and you can suddenly find yourself worried about how it's all going to come together. Take plenty of time to assess your needs and craft a design before starting construction to build your confidence about the finished product.

Talk with your contractor about job-site rules and expectations.
Before construction begins, discuss expectations about worker behavior. For example, are you OK with smoking on the job site? Can any type of music be played, and what volume is acceptable? Will workers take off their shoes or wear protective booties over their shoes to avoid tracking in dirt, mud, and dust? How much cleanup are workers expected to do? Also ask about typical work schedules so you'll know when to expect workers to show up at your door.

Establish a project timeline.
Whether you are doing the work yourself or hiring a general contractor, outline the sequence of each step of the project, and note who will be doing the work and what materials are needed. If you have a plan in place, you can ensure all products are on site when they're ready to be installed and avoid uncertainty and confusion.

Take steps to control dust.
There's virtually no way to eliminate dust at a construction site, but you can successfully minimize it. Seal off work areas with plastic sheeting, and set up an entrance for workers so they don't have to disturb the hanging plastic or tramp through the rest of the house. During the remodeling project, plan to clean the rest of your house frequently— construction dust is fine and can find its way through even the best protection. Also consider getting your home's ductwork cleaned after construction is done.

Keep kids safe.
Power tools, stacks of lumber, and exposed electrical wires pose serious dangers for children. Ask workers to put tools away, and plan to shut and lock doors when possible. Extra trips to the park, library, or Grandma's house can also help keep kids out of harm's way.

Design a temporary kitchen.
If you're remodeling your kitchen, plan to move the refrigerator, microwave, coffeemaker, and a few other often-used appliances into another room where you can still use them. And don't forget to consider how you'll clean up after your meals. If washing dishes in the bathroom sounds unappealing, you might want to stock up on disposable plates and utensils.

Set up a communication center.
Put up a message board at the job site where you and your contractor can leave questions and comments about the day's work. Also establish a consistent day and time for project meetings with your team to discuss work progress, weekly schedules, and any unexpected discoveries.

Protect valuables.
Hopefully you trust the workers you decide to hire, but keep in mind that all the hammering and demolition work can cause what feels like minor earthquakes in your house. If you have prized collections or delicate objects in your kitchen or bath (or an adjacent room), pack them away until construction work is done.

Create dedicated storage space for construction materials.
Whether you are acting as your own general contractor or have hired someone else to handle this task, you can avoid project delays by ordering materials in advance. But you'll need a place to store all the lumber and materials, so choose a safe place and clean out the area in advance.

floor plan ideas

These kitchen and bath layouts can help you maximize comfort and efficiency. Choose a standard floor plan that suits your space—then personalize it to make it your own.

galley kitchen

Perfect for tight quarters, this one- or two-wall kitchen layout makes the most of limited space with a compact work triangle that puts everything within easy reach of the cook.

A galley kitchen may be small, but there's reason to celebrate. Its efficient design helps the cook take fewer steps when preparing meals. In two-wall designs, place two points of the work triangle (see shaded area on the floor plan) on one wall and the third point on the other. In many cases, it works best to put the sink and refrigerator on the same wall and the cooktop opposite. In single-wall layouts, center the sink between the refrigerator and cooktop; allow ample counter space on either side of the sink for food prep and cleanup.

Improve traffic flow with a wide aisle—at least 4 feet—if more than one person is working at the same time. Help your kitchen work harder by consolidating counter space near appliances used most often. Maximize storage potential with upper cabinets that reach to the ceiling, a pullout pantry tower, or satellite storage in an adjacent room.

To help a galley kitchen feel larger, use light wood tones and paint colors. Open shelving, glass-front cabinet doors, and large exterior windows also reduce that boxed-in feeling.

TUCKED AWAY in the corner, a cooktop and hood, *above*, handle cooking duties with sleek, contemporary style. Cabinets with an open toe-kick help to visually expand the room.

SLEEK STYLE can give a small kitchen fresh allure. Slab-front cabinets with a faux zebrawood laminate and horizontal graining, *right*, keep the eye moving.

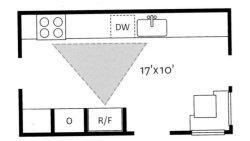

17'x10'

USE GLASS to visually expand a small kitchen. A French door and large windows amplify natural light, *above*.

PLACE YOUR FRIDGE near a doorway to keep snack-grabbing kids outside the work core. A side panel on the refrigerator, *far left*, adds a custom look.

A COZY BANQUETTE pairs with a petite table, *left*, to create an inviting dining space.

L-shape kitchen

A flexible work triangle with workstations on intersecting walls makes this layout popular. It can accommodate multiple cooks and opens the kitchen to adjacent living areas.

Hardworking L-shape layouts put two workstations on one wall and a single workstation on the adjacent wall. (See the shaded work triangle on the floor plan.) This layout works best in a 10×10-foot or larger room that lets you route traffic out of the L's crook. Arrange appliances and fixtures to suit the way you cook; if possible, place the refrigerator near the eating area so guests can grab drinks without interrupting the cook.

L-shape kitchens can serve a single cook or multiple cooks with ease, especially when outfitted with a center island or table. Include a prep sink or cooktop in the island, and you'll create two overlapping work triangles that streamline kitchen tasks. Extend the island's countertop, and you've also got a convenient spot for casual dining, homework supervision, and guest seating during parties.

LONG STRETCHES of countertop flanking the sink, *right,* allow multiple cooks to help with food prep and cleanup. Put the end of the island to work with a towel bar or built-in shelving for cookbooks.

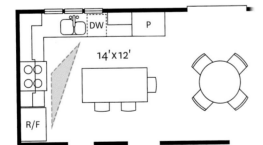

14' X 12'

Safety Tips
FOLLOW THESE GUIDELINES TO ENSURE YOUR KITCHEN IS SAFE FOR ALL USERS.

Add proper lighting. Good general lighting and glare-free task lights focused on work surfaces decrease the chance of injuries.

Install slip-resistant flooring. Matte-finish wood or laminates, textured vinyl, or grouted tile help prevent falls. Throw rugs should have nonskid backing.

Avoid sharp corners. Choose rounded corners for islands and peninsulas to avoid painful collisions—especially if you have young children.

Make the microwave convenient. Locate the microwave oven at a height that doesn't require reaching up to retrieve hot food.

ADDING AN ISLAND makes this kitchen's work triangle more efficient by providing a central spot for food prep, *above*. Wide aisles (42 inches or more is best) improve traffic flow.

COOKING IS CONCENTRATED on one leg of the L-shape layout, with a microwave oven installed above the range, *far left*. The refrigerator (not shown) is just a step away to ensure convenience.

SMART STORAGE outside the work core can keep food, small appliances, and bulky cookware organized. This floor-to-ceiling pantry cabinet, *left*, is positioned at the end of one wall, serving as a subtle divider between the kitchen and eating area.

U-shape kitchen

With one workstation on each wall, a U-shape kitchen delivers an efficient work triangle that saves steps for the primary cook yet allows for kitchen helpers.

The smart and versatile U-shape kitchen layout puts one workstation on each of its three walls (see shaded area on the floor plan). That means the cook is just a quick turn away from the next task. It also means (if the kitchen is large enough) that a second cook can prepare food at the same time by sharing a leg of the work triangle. This plan works best if the base of the U is at least 8 feet long. Often the sink is found at the base of the U, with the range and fridge across from each other on opposite walls—but it's really just a matter of personal preference.

Adding an island makes it even easier for multiple cooks to share kitchen duties— especially if the island includes a cooktop or a second sink to anchor multiple work triangles. In this setup, arrange workstations on adjacent walls so you don't have to constantly walk around the island. Plan at least 42 inches of space on all sides of the island (or 48 inches in a two-cook kitchen) to prevent traffic jams.

CENTRALIZE MEAL-PLANNING and bill-paying with a handy desk, *above*, at the edge of a U-shape plan. This approach makes sit-down tasks convenient without intruding into work zones.

A HALF-WALL topped with a counter, *right*, offers a comfy spot for dining. This setup also helps the compact kitchen feel larger by providing views into the adjacent room.

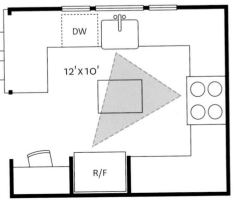

SMALL BUT MIGHTY, a table-turned-island, *left*, serves as an extra work space and landing zone. Large windows, open-display storage, and glass-front cabinet doors lighten the look. To make the most of corner cabinets, consider installing lazy Susans or swing-out shelves that make items easier to reach.

two-island kitchen

Make the most of your spacious kitchen with dual islands that can streamline cooking tasks and provide additional space for casual dining.

Are you planning an extra-large kitchen because you love to cook for a crowd or want to make a grand statement when you entertain? Consider installing two islands to streamline kitchen tasks. Unlike one large island that can become a barrier to traffic flow, two islands can help you save steps and time while preparing meals. Putting a second sink, a cooktop, or refrigerator drawers in one of the islands creates a compact work triangle when paired with a range and refrigerator on the perimeter. The extra sink or appliance can also become part of overlapping work triangles (see shaded areas on the floor plan), which allow you to more easily accommodate multiple cooks. By designating a second island for casual dining, you'll enhance the kitchen's status as the heart of the home. Guests can stay out of the way but easily converse with the chef. The island's big sweep of countertop is also a perfect spot for kids to do homework or for serving meals buffet-style.

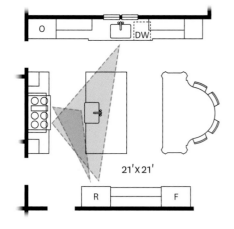

21'X 21'

FOOD PREP begins at this well-equipped island, *above,* just a pivot away from the main sink, the refrigerator, and the range on the three perimeter walls.

BECAUSE OF ITS SIZE, this 450-square-foot kitchen, *right,* includes two islands: one with a curved overhang designed for sitting and eating, and a second island by the range that anchors the main work zone.

two-island kitchen

AN APPLIANCE GARAGE, *above left*, conceals the espresso machine. Put this specialty appliance next to the refrigerator or wine chiller to create a convenient beverage center.

CUSTOM STORAGE between twin refrigerators, *above*, creates dedicated space for food, entertaining supplies, small appliances, and a television. Contrasting finishes on the island and perimeter cabinets break up the room visually.

GLASS-FRONT DOORS reveal root vegetables in bins below the wall unit's granite countertop, *far left*.

ELEGANT DETAILS, such as carved corbels on the dining island's corners, *left*, add furniture-style sophistication that helps the kitchen transition into an adjoining living space.

Add seating. Extend one island's countertop to create a comfortable spot for dining; plan to allow 24 inches of width per person.

Include ventilation. If you have a cooktop in your island, install a sculptural chimney hood or an unobtrusive downdraft ventilation system to carry away smoke and odors.

Boost island storage. Consider adding extra-deep drawers for pots; vertical slots for baking sheets; drawer inserts for utensils; and open shelving for cookbooks.

Build in wide aisles. Plan to leave 48 inches of space around an island to help multiple cooks work comfortably and to ease traffic flow from adjoining rooms.

Add task lighting. Install one or more pendant lights above each island to illuminate busy work areas.

A FOCAL-POINT eight-burner cooktop gains presence from a large carved-stone hood, *left*. Keep elements in scale with the size of the room; larger kitchens may call for thicker countertops and taller cabinets.

three-quarter bath

Practical and hardworking, this layout with a shower but no bathtub is popular for hall bathrooms or where space is limited. It's a budget-friendly plan that's smart and streamlined.

When you want to squeeze a lot of function into a small space, a three-quarter bath is a great option. It generally includes only one sink, a toilet, and a shower—but no bathtub. Because it offers a bathing space (unlike a half bath), it's an ideal second bath for households with multiple people getting ready for school or work in the morning, but it does not necessarily require as much space as a full bath—particularly if the shower stall is small.

If you're designing a three-quarter bath, keep in mind that you can save money on labor and supplies by lining up all the plumbing fixtures on one wall. Also consider using light colors and glass surfaces to make a compact bath feel larger and more inviting. With careful planning, a three-quarter bath can be both smart and stylish.

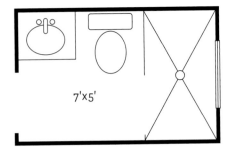

7'x5'

A COMPACT VANITY, *right,* offers efficient storage in a small footprint, and it's more practical than a pedestal sink in a busy family bath. When space is limited, consider installing a built-in medicine cabinet that's flush with the wall.

NEUTRAL HUES,
above, set a soothing tone in a small bath. Here, white subway tile references the 1920s heritage of the home, while gray paint on the walls and vanity keep the space from feeling too stark. A strip of black border tile unifies the shower and the rest of the room.

BUILT-IN SHELVES,
above right, provide handy storage space in the shower for soap and shampoo. In a small bath, look for opportunities to add niches or open shelving between wall studs to make the most of the room's limited footprint.

A LARGE SHOWER,
right, takes full advantage of the space at the end of the room. This curbless shower is easily accessible and features a tiled floor that slopes toward the drain. The glass shower door swings in or out, making the bathroom feel more spacious.

combined tub and shower

This space-savvy floor plan includes a shower and bathtub in the same unit, increasing efficiency and versatility. Custom details upgrade the look in these hardworking baths.

Commonly found in shared hall baths, this floor plan maximizes function in a small space by combining the tub and shower into a single footprint. Such setups are often constructed from prefabricated kits made of fiberglass or acrylic, but you can easily personalize the look with upscale fixtures, custom tile, cultured marble sheets, a sliding glass shower door, or a stylish shower curtain.

To ensure two people can use the bath on busy mornings, consider including a large vanity with two sinks, two roomy grooming stations that share a single sink, or two separate vanities. Although you probably won't have space for a separate toilet room, consider hiding the toilet behind a half-wall or a privacy panel made of sandblasted tempered glass. Just putting the toilet off to one side of the doorway can elevate the look.

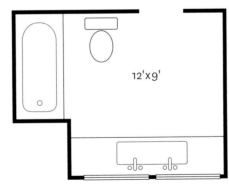

12'X9'

ONE TROUGH SINK with two wall-mount faucets and a large niche for bath staples, *right*, means two can get ready as quickly as one. Place a stylish vanity opposite the door for a dramatic entrance.

COMBINING A SHOWER with a deep soaking tub saves space without sacrificing style, *right*. Install a glass shower door to help a small space feel larger. Here, a half-width glass door contains spray but makes it easy to bathe small children.

A GENEROUS STRETCH of countertop on either side of the sink, *below*, gives each user personal space to place grooming gear. A wall-mount extendable mirror pulls in close to help with shaving, tweezing, and makeup application.

A TILED NICHE recessed between wall studs makes the most of otherwise-wasted space in the shower, *below right*. Lining the niche with the same green tile that's used for the wall's accent stripe turns the storage space into a graphic element.

Bath Safety
FOLLOW THESE TIPS TO DESIGN A BATH THAT'S SAFE FOR EVERYONE.

Ease entries into tub and shower areas. Eliminate steps by the shower, and include a wide tub surround so you can sit while getting in or out of the tub.

Install grab bars to prevent falls. For greater stability, make sure they're anchored to framing studs.

Use ground fault circuit interrupters. These electrical outlets shut off automatically when they sense moisture.

Prevent scalding. Install pressure-balanced and temperature-controlled shower valves, or set your water heater thermostat to 120°F or below.

Ensure adequate lighting. Add task lighting in the vanity area and shower for the day and a low light (such as a night-light) to illuminate the way at night.

Classic white cabinets and soft-green tile create a soothing, spa-like atmosphere.

separate tub and shower

This luxurious plan lets you relax and spread out, with distinct areas for showering and bathing. It streamlines morning routines by helping two people use the bath at the same time.

Space restrictions often influence how a master bath can be designed. If you're lucky enough to have ample square footage in your bathroom, indulge each partner by putting in a separate bathtub and shower.

For a medium-size bath, it makes sense to put the separate tub and shower side-by-side to save room and avoid the cost of running additional plumbing lines to each fixture. For a larger, more luxurious bathroom, spread out the two main fixtures. Place the tub where it can serve as a pretty focal point, either beneath a window or directly opposite the bath's main entrance. Dedicate space on another wall for a walk-in shower. Use the floor space between the two amenities for a large double vanity or two single vanities with personalized storage features that pair smart function and custom style.

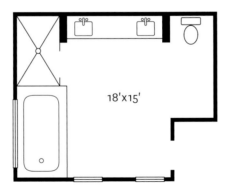

18'x15'

GLASS DOORS show off bookmarked slabs of marble in the shower, *right*, which is situated next to the tub. The shower door opens into the shower to avoid conflicts with the neighboring vanity.

AN 8-FOOT-LONG VANITY, *above,* adds sophisticated style and smart storage to the master bath. A glass partition separates the toilet area without blocking natural light.

DETAILED WOODWORK on the tub's surround, *far left,* matches the elegant look of the vanity and surrounding stone surfaces. Positioned at the side of the room, the tub basks in natural light admitted by the room's largest window.

POLISHED-NICKEL FIXTURES, *left,* sparkle above the tub's marble deck, which is wide enough to keep bath supplies within easy reach.

luxury bath

Sophisticated materials and high-end fixtures have room to shine in spacious bathrooms. With smart floor plans, these inviting retreats enhance both privacy and convenience.

So you're finally designing that spa-worthy master bathroom. Maybe you already have room to accommodate a walk-in shower and other dreamy features—if not, don't shy away from borrowing space from an adjoining bedroom closet. Individual amenities rule in these types of baths, especially if you have two people on the same morning schedule. Fit in both a large walk-in shower and a soaking tub for relaxing baths and romance. Put them on the same wall if needed; in a larger room, place each amenity where it will get the attention it deserves.

Build in roomy grooming stations, whether that means one long vanity with matching sinks or twin vanities. In each case, good vanity lighting and personalized storage features are a must. To enhance privacy, add a separate room for the toilet—and maybe a bidet, too. Add sophisticated sconces, a dreamy chandelier, or transom windows to illuminate the space and lighten the look.

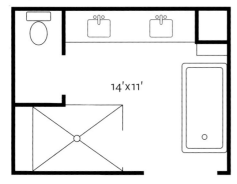

14'x11'

THREE-DIMENSIONAL AMBER TILES create an opulent backdrop for a sleek freestanding tub and tub filler, *above*. Keep the focus on a unique feature—without sacrificing function—by adding accessible storage (such as these wall-mount shelves) that melts into the background.

A DOUBLE VANITY crafted from white oak exudes luxury when paired with a wall and countertop of heavily veined onyx, *opposite*. Onyx is softer than granite and marble, but it offers dramatic color and veining for a distinctive look.

luxury bath

WALL-MOUNT CHROME FAUCETS, *above,* accent each vanity sink. Their placement leaves the entire countertop free for perfumes, lotions, and other everyday necessities.

AN ETCHED-GLASS DOOR opens to reveal the water closet's secret: a lush mural with hints of Art Nouveau styling, *right*. Crafting the aluminum-frame door with translucent glass instead of wood keeps the small room from feeling closed in.

AN ONYX BENCH and wall niche link the white-marble shower enclosure to the rest of the bathroom, *opposite*. Use grouted tiles (these are marble) to create a slip-resistant floor.

Indulgent Ideas

THESE SPA-WORTHY AMENITIES PROMISE TO HELP YOU RELAX.

Install an oversize walk-in shower. Add dual rain-style showerheads and hand showers, as well as a lineup of adjustable body sprays. Consider including a steam generator and operable transoms up top to let out steam when desired.

Choose a freestanding tub. Paired with a sculptural floor-mount tub filler, these tubs serve as a dramatic focal point. Choose one large enough for two bathers.

Add a dressing table. In addition to two sinks, consider including a dressing table at a lower height that's designed for putting on makeup. Position it under a window to take advantage of natural light.

Install a two-sided gas fireplace. Place it between the master bedroom and bath—or between the bath and an outdoor patio.

decorating styles

Focusing on a specific design style can help you create stunning spaces. Choose a look that feels right to you and complements the way you live.

traditional elegance

Distinctive architectural details and classic materials create a timeless beauty that's warm and inviting.

In traditional kitchens and baths, the beauty is in the details. Layered moldings, raised-panel cabinet doors, intricate carvings on custom range hoods, and decorative toe-kicks on cabinets catch the eye and encourage a closer look. Traditional rooms eschew the sleek lines of contemporary style in favor of graceful arches and gentle curves—or simply-detailed cabinet doors paired with stone countertops.

Whether you opt for a vintage look with classic subway tiles and bridge-style faucets or a more sophisticated space with elegant marble surfaces and glazed cabinet finishes, traditional kitchens and baths always feel warm and welcoming. Although they may have professional-style appliances or spa-like luxuries, these rooms aren't about showing off—they're meant to be lived in and enjoyed.

SUNNY YELLOW cabinets, *right*, bring instant warmth to this cooking zone. An apron-front sink, bridge-style faucet, and vintage pendant light add old-fashioned charm.

BEADED DETAILING on cabinet doors, fluted pilasters, and deep crown molding, *far right*, enhance this kitchen's traditional pedigree. A dark stain on the island adds contrast while maintaining a sophisticated, neutral color palette.

traditional elegance

Elements of Traditional Style

THESE CLASSIC FEATURES ADD WELCOMING WARMTH.

Elegant architectural details. Add deep crown molding, coffered ceilings, and carved designs or molding on cabinet doors and custom range hoods.

Furniture-style elements. Include a hutch or buffet to amplify storage. Conceal modern appliances behind cabinet panels or in a furniture-look armoire.

Natural materials. Granite, marble, and wood surfaces add classic charm and warmth.

Traditional tile treatments. Add authentic character with vintage-look subway or hexagonal tile.

Old-fashioned fixtures. Claw-foot tubs, farmhouse sinks, and curvy faucets look right at home in traditional rooms.

THE RANGE HOOD, *above*, serves as a stunning focal point, thanks to its hearth-style design and eye-catching limestone and copper materials. Slate tile laid in a harlequin pattern brings soft color to the backsplash, while glazed white cabinets give the new kitchen instant age.

CONTRASTING FINISHES and countertop materials, *right*, help set off the island work zone and lend visual interest to the cooking zone. Exposed wood beams on the ceiling complement the wood floor and add a rustic touch that enhances the kitchen's warmth.

traditional elegance baths

A FREESTANDING TUB and generous shower, *left*, take center stage in this master bath. An octagonal tile "rug" around the tub anchors the bathing space and adds detail underfoot. Glass walls show off the dual showerheads and custom tile mural while enhancing the shower's spacious feel.

AN UPHOLSTERED CHAIR anchors an elegant grooming area, *below left*. Celadon green cabinets are glazed with a pale chocolate hue to achieve an aged patina, while green onyx dots add subtle color and interest to the basket-weave floor.

HONED MARBLE wraps the soaking tub and floor in luxury, *below*. Large-format tiles keep the stone's pattern from becoming too busy, while a soft blue paint on the walls brings subtle color to the primarily black-and-white decor. A symmetrical layout centered around the focal-point tub complements the room's traditional style.

cottage chic

Showcasing vintage charm and soft colors, cottage-style kitchens and baths are cheerful and inviting—encouraging you to celebrate the simple pleasures of everyday life.

Practical and comfortable, cottage-style kitchens and baths encourage you to relax and stay awhile with their quiet charm and cozy demeanor. They celebrate the beauty of traditional architecture with vintage accents and classic fixtures, but avoid fussy details in favor of clean lines and simple forms that promise to stand the test of time. These pretty and efficient rooms look light and airy thanks to their focus on bright whites and soft colors—but a pop of bright color here and there often adds a playful vibe. Natural materials, such as traditional wood floors, keep these spaces grounded and enhance their warmth and character. With an understated elegance, cottage-style rooms offer a relaxed feel that's just right for everyday living and casual entertaining.

CHEERFUL YELLOW PAINT on custom cabinets, *right,* warms up a hardworking cooking zone with vintage-style details. The pine floor and mix of maple and stone countertops enhance the room's casual tone that seamlessly blends old and new.

CLASSIC WHITE CABINETRY, *opposite,* is adorned with vintage-style bin pulls and paired with an extra-deep farmhouse sink to create a cooking area with old-fashioned charm. Decorative brackets add character to shelves on the sink wall.

Elements of Cottage Style

CHARMING SIMPLICITY RULES IN THESE ROOMS.

Open shelving. Install wall shelves with decorative brackets to lighten the look in a small kitchen and add informal charm. Or take off the doors of a few upper cabinets and paint the back of the cabinets with a cheerful hue.

Painted cabinets with Shaker-style doors. These simple and elegant cabinets mix traditional details and clean lines. They're often painted white to enhance the kitchen's open and airy feel.

Beaded-board details. Install wainscoting in the bathroom, or choose cabinets with beaded-board doors in the kitchen. For a more modern look, consider using whitewashed horizontal paneling.

Vintage-style fixtures and hardware. Think faucets with cross handles and apron-front sinks. Bin-style drawer pulls and glass knobs also add old-fashioned style.

Claw-foot tubs. These freestanding tubs double as a sculptural focal point. Refinish or paint a salvaged tub, or opt for a new lightweight model.

Playful accents. Add a bold dash of color with paint or a fun floral fabric for a modern twist on cottage style.

cottage chic

A CHECKERBOARD FLOOR, *left*, adds vibrant energy and a vintage feel to a kitchen dressed in neutral tones. The mossy-hue island with open shelves offers easy access to entertaining staples and everyday cookware.

A VINTAGE CAST-IRON SINK anchors this compact but efficient kitchen, *below left*. Glass-front cabinets help to visually expand the small space, and a minty-fresh paint color adds playful appeal.

OPEN SHELVES show off a collection of colorful dinnerware, *below*, for a dash of cheerful color. Golden fir lower cabinets lend rustic charm, while upper cabinets extend to the countertop, enhancing storage and leaving space for a small window above.

Bold dashes of color showcase cottage style's playful spirit, while white backdrops keep the overall look light and airy.

cottage chic baths

BRIGHT BLUE WALLS, *left,* contrast with sophisticated marble surfaces and give this upscale bath its playful, cottage feel. A console table with dual sinks retains an open feeling in the vanity area to visually expand the space. Tall mirrors and sleek sconces with mirrored backplates reflect light and views throughout the room.

SUBWAY TILE on the walls, *below left,* sets a charmingly vintage tone in this small bath. A pedestal sink and claw-foot tub complement the look, while a painted table, vibrant rug, and colorful collectibles add a fun cottage vibe.

A PAINTED CABINET displaying towels and grooming supplies, *below,* adds a furniture element that upgrades this bath's overall style. A wide console sink combines old-fashioned charm with a practical landing space for everyday necessities.

country french warmth

Embrace the welcoming balance that comes from creatively mixing casual and elegant elements.

Kitchens and baths that showcase country French elements promise to always be in style—thanks to their warm ambience, uninhibitedly cheerful colors, heirloom furniture treasured by generations, rough-and-tumble sturdiness, and unflappable *joie de vivre*. A mix of wood and stone creates a beautiful framework for these rooms and provides compelling natural texture that grounds the space. Distressed finishes bring timeworn elegance that gracefully connects the room to days gone by, while romantic flourishes add softness and charming detail.

HEFTY WOOD BEAMS and textural plaster walls, *right*, lend this kitchen an authentic aged look. Richly-detailed cabinets and an ironwork chandelier showcase the style's decorative flourishes, and an antique table with turned legs adds informal charm.

THE LIGHTER SIDE of country French style is on display in this airy white kitchen, *far right*, with creamy-color walls and white marble countertops. A curvaceous stucco hood and antique chandeliers add romance, while a salvaged pantry door and rustic floor provide natural texture.

Elements of Country French Style

USE RUSTIC ACCENTS TO INJECT TIMELESS CHARM.

Cabinetry in a variety of woods and painted finishes. Go with distressed finishes for a gathered-over-time look. Islands sometimes boast a bright color.

Hand-plastered walls. These textural walls are often painted in neutral colors such as white, cream, and pale yellow. These colors may deepen into golden hues for additional drama.

Tiled backsplashes. Try aged brick and mortar; pale, mottled limestone; or checked patterns in primary blues and yellows. Or use glossy white tile for a charming bistro look.

Natural surfaces. Consider ceilings with beams in rough aged woods. Install rustic flooring of hand-scraped wood, brick, limestone, or terra-cotta tile.

Hardware with an aged-bronze finish. Choose cabinet pulls in a twisted-rope style, scrolled knobs, and iron pot racks.

Rustic furnishings. Add a timeworn country table with mismatched chairs or a bureau repurposed as a vanity. Include open shelving for collectibles.

Provencal fabrics. Opt for toiles, plaids, stripes, and checks in primary colors such as deep yellow, royal blue, and bright red.

county french warmth

Timeworn finishes and collectibles give country French kitchens personal appeal.

WARM HUES introduce charm, *above*. The kitchen's authentic country French mix includes roughly plastered golden walls, a French range in Provence yellow, a range hood finished in a faux-aged copper, and an island painted in classic French blue. Unmatched cabinetry finishes and a hammered-copper sink also add authenticity.

DISTRESSED CABINETS painted a pale blue, *left*, add instant age and warmth to this compact cooking zone. An antique fireplace mantel found in France serves as an eye-catching range hood, while a narrow farm table stands in for an island. Limestone flooring and backsplash tiles provide soft color and texture.

country french baths

A SCULPTURAL TUB gets star treatment in front of a bay window, *left,* enhancing the bathroom's timeless style. Floor-length draperies soften the basket-weave marble floor, while a crystal chandelier adds sparkle and drama overhead.

NEUTRAL HUES and traditional wood cabinetry give this vanity area, *below left,* a sophisticated tone. Rectangular sinks add a touch of modern elegance, while tile wainscoting brings soft pattern and classic charm to the walls.

GRANITE-TOPPED VANITIES flank a soaking tub in this elegant retreat, *below.* A black-and-white stone floor and traditional tub filler hearken to days gone by, while a painted chandelier and soft curtains at the window add the romantic details associated with country French style.

contemporary glamour

Clean, sleek, and uncluttered, today's modern designs are anything but ordinary. The bold style brings drama and showstopping appeal to hardworking kitchens and baths.

Free from fuss, contemporary kitchens and baths boast an exciting mix of sophisticated materials and smart function. Abiding by the philosophy of "less is more," the best contemporary spaces emphasize quality over quantity, minimizing ornamentation in favor of clean lines, square profiles, streamlined faucets, sleek appliances, and sculptural tubs. But within this unadorned framework, surprises abound. Bold lighting, dramatic architecture, high-tech features, and an occasional pop of vibrant color add plenty of personality to these one-of-a-kind rooms.

SHIMMERY BACKSPLASH TILE accented by simple wood shelves, *right,* creates a stunning focal point amid streamlined white cabinetry. A terrazzo floor lends visual interest underfoot—and its lively pattern helps to hide scuffs and dirt.

GLASS AND METAL combine with natural wood to create an industrial chic cooking space, *opposite,* that still feels warm and welcoming. Beneath the dramatic A-frame architecture, a ceiling-piercing hood and sculptural-quality hanging lights catch the eye. A mix of high-gloss metal and flat-front walnut cabinets celebrate contemporary design's focus on sleek simplicity, while honed marble countertops introduce the classic appeal of natural stone.

Elements of Modern Style

SIMPLE FORMS AND SLEEK LINES ADD A CONTEMPORARY VIBE.

Eurostyle, full-overlay cabinets. These streamlined door styles can be finished in laminate, metal, or wood veneer for a chic look. Enhance visual interest with frosted-glass inserts.

Deep drawers. Used instead of—or in addition to—conventional kitchen cabinets, drawers offer smart storage space and emphasize this style's focus on horizontal lines.

Sleek sinks. Opt for undermount kitchen sinks with single-handle or commercial-style faucets. In the bath, try rectangular basins with single-lever or wall-mount faucets.

Rectilinear backsplash tiles. Often made of glass, these tiles introduce sleek style and a touch of drama.

Metallic accents. Go with stainless-steel appliances and sculptural, chimney-style range hoods. Enhance cabinets with oversize bar pulls in stainless steel or polished chrome.

Dramatic lighting. Use track lights or simple pendants with geometric shapes in the kitchen and sleek sconces in the bath.

Open floor plans. These smart layouts seamlessly integrate the kitchen with the home's living areas.

contemporary glamour

Sculptural focal points lend drama and intrigue amid streamlined forms and clean lines.

DRESSED IN WHITE, this sophisticated kitchen, *left*, combines classic materials—a marble backsplash and counters—with modern fixtures, such as sleek-front cabinets in high-gloss laminate and stainless-steel appliances and accents.

BOLD COLOR highlights an eating bar in a condo kitchen, *above*. Tubular stainless-steel pulls accent the frameless cabinets, and hefty honed-granite countertops pair practicality and style in the work zone.

contemporary glamour baths

EYE-CATCHING CURVES earn a place in contemporary design, too. An egg-shape tub, *left*, serves as a sculptural focal point amid the room's busy tile patterns. A sleek floor-mount tub filler includes a handy shelf for bathing necessities.

GLOSSY WHITE LAMINATE adds modern flair to a floating vanity, *below left*. Marble liner tiles dress the wall, continuing the bathroom's focus on sleek lines, while flared rims on rectangular vessel sinks transform everyday fixtures into artwork.

LIMESTONE LINER TILES, *below,* create a striking horizontal band of tile that wraps around the room. An angular soaking tub celebrates contemporary design's focus on streamlined forms, while neutral limestone tiles add a natural look and texture underfoot.

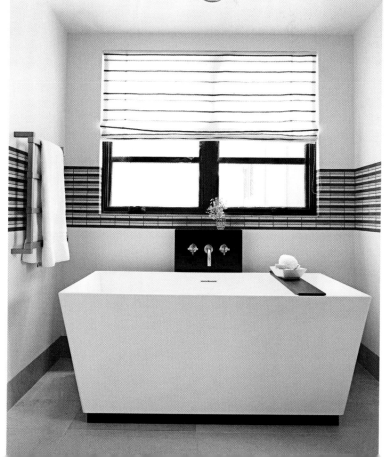

transitional beauty

Combining a little of this and a little of that,
transitional spaces blend the best elements of contemporary and traditional design for a winning style all their own.

Can't decide between the warmth and elegance of traditional style or the sleek sophistication of contemporary designs? Transitional style—which blends elements from both styles—may be the perfect fit. Because it's a hybrid, a transitional kitchen or bath complements a range of house styles and allows you the opportunity to creatively mix materials and forms without abiding by rigid design rules. You may choose to combine high-gloss finishes or stainless-steel appliances with classic stone surfaces, for example, or add a sleek light fixture to a room with simply-styled, traditional cabinetry. The unexpected charms found in a transitional kitchen or bathroom reflect a bit of the past, a bit of the future, and a whole lot of you—creating a signature look sure to delight both you and your guests.

A PRO-STYLE RANGE and sleek hood, *right*, add a surprisingly modern note to a kitchen with vintage-style open shelving, marble countertops, and traditional cabinets with old-fashioned bin pulls. The checkerboard floor lends a playful energy to the space.

TRADITIONAL CABINETS, *far right*, show off the simple lines and detailing often found in transitional rooms. An old-fashioned chandelier is juxtaposed with a shiny tile backsplash for a unique look. Windows behind glass-front cabinets amplify light.

transitional beauty

GLOSSY GLASS TILES modernize the classic subway tile format, *above,* while an espresso-stained island features a furniture look that recalls the handcrafted charm of historical homes. A durable quartz-surfacing countertop unites the room's brown and green hues.

BOLD RED PAINT on Shaker-style cabinets, *right,* adds fresh energy to a classic farmhouse-style kitchen. Distressed-wood furniture recalls country kitchens, open shelving lends vintage charm, and cable lights and industrial-style pendants add modern style and function.

A WALNUT-AND-STAINLESS-STEEL ISLAND, *far right,* along with shimmering backsplash tile, introduce sleek, contemporary style in a room with traditional cabinets and muted hues.

transitional beauty baths

A HONED-MARBLE COUNTERTOP and a footed base, *left,* set a traditional tone at this elegant vanity. But square-shape sconces and clean-lined cabinet doors nudge the room in a contemporary direction. Silvery finishes unite vintage-style faucets and oval cabinet knobs.

A CREAMY PALETTE and floor-length silk draperies, *below left,* create a romantic backdrop for a sculptural egg-shape tub. An old-fashioned handheld shower is juxtaposed with the sleek tub for a surprising mix of old and new.

GLAMOROUS ACCENTS and masculine elements meld seamlessly in this unique bath, *below.* A luxurious vanity boasts a streamlined rectangular sink as well as a wall-mount faucet with traditional cross handles. Olive grass-cloth wallcovering and traditional wood paneling add living room style for a formal and sophisticated look.

smart storage

Hardworking cabinets and custom shelving in the kitchen and bathroom allow you to create a place for everything—and help you easily find what you need.

kitchens

baths

cabinet solutions

Maximize kitchen storage space with stylish cabinets outfitted with custom inserts and convenient features. They'll help you enhance efficiency and accessibility in your work zone.

Kitchen cabinets make up a large percentage of any kitchen remodeling budget, so it's important to carefully consider both style and function when shopping. Take time to think about how you'll use the kitchen, and plan storage accordingly—making sure you can store items near where they will be used to save steps during meal preparation and cleanup.

Look for cabinets with organizational inserts (or add inserts to existing cabinets if you'll be keeping them in place) that make contents easy to access and make the best use of available storage space. Whether it's a slim pullout cabinet for spices near the range or a tilt-out drawer for sponges under the sink, smart storage features can have a huge impact on the everyday livability of your kitchen and help streamline cooking tasks. With careful planning, you can have everything right at your fingertips—right when you need it.

CUSTOM-FITTED PEGS hold dishware in a drawer, *far left*. This ergonomic setup ensures that setting the table is easy for helpers, regardless of their age or mobility.

A PULLOUT PANTRY, *left,* offers abundant storage space within a narrow footprint. Wire rails prevent items from falling off the shelves and make it easy to grab what's needed.

A CORNER STORAGE UNIT, *opposite,* features shelves that pull out and to the side—revealing a secondary storage space. With this handy setup, nothing gets lost in dark corners.

cabinet solutions

A BAKING CENTER includes a mixer lift installed within a base cabinet, *right*. Attached to a custom shelf in the cabinet, it lets you easily access the mixer when you need it—and hide it away when you don't.

CUSTOMIZED INSERTS maximize storage in a deep drawer, *below*. A top compartment slides out to reveal dividers for cooking utensils and built-in slots for knives. Lids are stored in the space below.

V-SHAPE CUSTOM DRAWERS, *bottom*, add handy storage to a tricky corner space.

A COMPACT PANTRY hidden behind a barn-look door, *above*, pairs smart pullouts and drawers for snacks, canned goods, and more. Before selecting a pantry cabinet, carefully measure your space. A pullout cabinet is a great choice for a small kitchen, while reach-in pantries outfitted with shallow shelves work well in larger rooms.

SHALLOW DRAWERS built into the base of a vintage-style hutch, *above right*, keep table linens organized and easily accessible. Place storage for entertaining essentials near your formal dining area and out of the way of the primary cooking zone to streamline party prep.

A SLIM PULLOUT next to the range, *right*, keeps spices close at hand and makes smart use of a few extra inches of cabinet space. Plus, it helps eliminate unsightly gaps around the range, where food can fall between the stove and surrounding cabinets. Traditional moldings on the front of the pullout disguise its hardworking nature and enhance the kitchen's elegant style.

cabinet solutions

SLEEK UPPER CABINETS hinge at the top, *right*, to offer unimpeded access to the dishes inside. Frosted-glass doors partially conceal contents while maintaining an open and airy look.

A THREE-TIER SHELF, *below,* ensures cooking oils, spices, and utensils can be easily accessed—and seen—all at once.

A TAMBOUR DOOR, *below right,* conceals small appliances when they're not in use. Include an outlet inside the countertop garage so you can hide cord clutter and more easily use appliances.

VERTICAL SLOTS built into an island, *below, far right,* keep cutting boards upright and within easy reach. Use vertical dividers inside cabinets to organize serving trays and baking sheets as well.

CUTLERY BINS inside a deep drawer, *opposite,* make it easy to grab the silverware you need. Consider placing the silverware drawer near your family's informal eating area to streamline table-setting chores and encourage kids to help.

Smart Ways to Boost Storage

USE THESE CLEVER TRICKS TO PACK EXTRA FUNCTION INTO YOUR SMALL KITCHEN.

- Put cabinet toe-kicks to work. Use the space below cabinets to store serving platters or baking sheets—or hide the dog food bowl.
- Add storage above the refrigerator. Install wine cubbies that are both decorative and functional, or add a cabinet for items you use infrequently.
- Extend cabinets to the ceiling. Consider adding glass-front cabinets along the top of the room to display favorite collectibles or serving trays.
- Install slim pullout cabinets to fill gaps between larger cabinets. Rather than using filler strips, put these few extra inches of space to work with spice racks or knife and utensil holders.
- Add slim storage inserts inside drawers. This strategy can double the available storage space and works well for cutlery, pot lids, or other small kitchen tools.

pantry ideas

Add efficient storage for dry goods with a walk-in pantry that pairs smart features and designer looks. Here's what to consider when creating your perfect pantry.

Walk-in pantries—those spacious storage rooms coveted by organized cooks everywhere—offer a convenient spot for storing bulk goods and large quantities of food items. Ideally, they can store at least a week's worth of groceries. Because of their size, they're often located in a room adjacent to the kitchen rather than in the middle of the cooking zone, but it's important to make sure they are easily accessible from the food preparation area—or supplemented by a smaller pullout pantry in the kitchen. If your current kitchen doesn't have space for a walk-in pantry, look for an extra closet or a corner of another room that can be converted into an efficient pantry space.

Inside the pantry, combine open shelving and cabinetry to create versatile storage for groceries, as well as small appliances and entertaining supplies. To enhance convenience, make sure everything is easily visible—rather than hidden behind other items—or group similar items in decorative bins or baskets. Consider including shallow shelves in at least one area of the pantry; these can help ensure canned goods and other small items don't get lost in the back. Also look for ways to use the back of the door to maximize storage space.

A FROSTED-GLASS DOOR slides open to reveal custom shelving for dry goods, *right*. Vary the height of shelves to accommodate a range of items, and use clear canisters to make items easy to find.

VERSATILE STORAGE in this stylish pantry, *left,* includes built-in wine racks, vertical slots for baking sheets, and drawers for table linens. Measure pots and pans before building shelves to make sure you have room for all your favorite cookware.

A CARVED WOOD DOOR, *below,* conceals the pantry and complements the kitchen's cabinetry for a sophisticated look. Painted cabinets in your pantry can continue your kitchen's decorative style and unify the two spaces.

A COUNTERTOP WORK SPACE, *bottom,* allows this pantry to serve as an extra prep zone, as well as a handy storage space. A mix of open shelving and drawers provides a convenient home for glassware, cutlery, cookware, and dry goods.

open shelving

Lighten your kitchen's look and add charm with stylish shelves and built-in cubbies that provide display space as well as a chance to introduce color and personality.

Kitchens jam-packed with cabinets offer tons of useful storage space, but sometimes they can look too, well, kitcheny. Replacing a few upper cabinets with open shelves—or just taking off the doors—can provide visual relief and lighten the overall look. This strategy is ideal for small kitchens but can be used anywhere to enhance a room's vintage charm and showcase favorite collectibles that help make your kitchen your own.

Of course open shelves also make everyday items more easily accessible, because there's no cabinet door to open and close. Consider using shelves near the sink or range to hold everyday dishes, or add open storage to an island to keep pots and pans or cookbooks within reach. Add open shelves where they make the most sense to you—and celebrate the informal charm they bring to your kitchen.

DECORATIVE BRACKETS, *right,* dress up simple pine shelves that are painted white. A display of white dishes keeps the overall look clean and sophisticated.

REMOVING CABINET DOORS enhances this kitchen's open and airy look and shows off colorful dishware, *far right*. Chalkboard paint and hand-written labels add charm at the back of the cabinets.

OPEN SHELVES added to the side of the island, *above*, create a pretty display space in an otherwise unused area. Turned legs and arched openings enhance architectural appeal.

STYLISH CUBBIES built into the back of this island, *far left*, can store up to 54 bottles of wine. Add wine storage or create a small bar area close to the entertaining zone but out of the main work area so guests can help themselves to drinks.

BUILT-IN BOOKSHELVES flank an eating area at this wenge-wood-topped island, *left*—creating handy storage space for cookbooks and collectibles. Petite corbels add ornate detail and complement the kitchen's traditional style.

stylish vanities

Whatever your favorite decorative style, smart storage is always in vogue—especially at a hardworking bathroom vanity. Make the most of your space with these clever design ideas.

Your bathroom vanity helps set the tone for the room—but even more importantly, it usually serves as the centerpiece storage element, holding toiletries, grooming tools, towels, and more. Think carefully about the storage features you'll want as you're choosing or designing your vanity. What exactly do you need to store there? Do you want items you use daily to be out in the open or hidden away behind closed doors? Or do you prefer the best of both worlds with a combination of open and closed storage?

Also look for storage inserts that enhance organization and ensure grooming essentials are easy to find on busy mornings. Pullout shelves, for example, make sure items don't get lost in the back of the vanity cabinet. Sliding compartments or customizable dividers in drawers keep small items organized and make the most of available space. And under-the-sink storage inserts can utilize valuable space around plumbing lines.

A RAISED CENTER CABINET, *right,* prevents this vanity's wall-to-wall countertop from becoming a cluttered runway. Outlets are hidden inside the cabinet's drawers to enhance convenience, and the center door conceals a large trash basket.

OPEN STORAGE for towels lightens the look of this countertop-to-ceiling cabinet, *above left*. The cabinet divides the vanity's two sink areas and adds handy storage for everyday grooming supplies.

A TILT-OUT DRAWER with a metal liner, *above*, holds a toothbrush and other daily essentials. Originally designed for the kitchen, the cabinet was repurposed for the bath.

PULLOUT SHELVES, *far left*, ensure that grooming supplies are easy to reach. A wire wine cooler corrals hairstyling tools, and a ceramic egg container prevents jewelry from becoming tangled.

BACK-OF-THE-DOOR STORAGE enhances available space in this vanity cabinet, *left*. Consider adding hooks or caddies that hang over the door.

stylish vanities

AN OPEN BASE keeps this vanity's contents in view, *left*—and within easy reach. Steel bars and cedar planks give the vanity rustic charm, while stylish baskets attractively corral frequently used toiletries.

SLIM DRAWERS pull out from within a custom wood vanity, *above*, ensuring sundries are organized and accessible but discreetly out of sight.

A PULLOUT HAMPER tucks into a handsome vanity, *below*. Look for a model with a basket that lifts out to make laundry chores easier.

A COHESIVE STORAGE PLAN gives this vanity area a sophisticated look, *opposite*. The stylish wood vanity is paired with a matching shelf that's just deep enough for displaying collectibles—but shallow enough to not interfere with grooming tasks. Open storage space under the sink offers additional display space and keeps towels close at hand, while drawers hide less-attractive items.

Easy Storage Upgrades

ADD EXTRA STORAGE TO YOUR BATH WITH THESE LOW-COST, NO-FUSS REMODELING IDEAS.

- Put wall space to work with wall-hung caddies for toothbrushes above the vanity or a floating shelf for towels under a console sink.
- Add freestanding cabinets to make use of vertical storage space. Vintage-style models pair glass-front cabinets for display and drawers for hardworking storage—enhancing both charm and function.
- Create a convenient spot for towels and robes. Add space-savvy hooks or prop a vintage ladder against the wall for easy-to-reach towel storage.
- Add smart storage to the backs of cabinet doors with over-the-door caddies that can organize often-used grooming essentials or cleaning supplies.
- Install shelf risers in the medicine cabinet or hanging baskets in the linen closet to make the most of available storage space between shelves.

built-in storage

Stylish niches, shelves, and cubbies give your bathroom a custom look and provide additional space for storing grooming supplies or displaying collectibles.

Even small bathrooms can enjoy ample storage if you look for creative ways to supplement vanity storage with built-in features. The space between wall studs offers an excellent spot for built-in shelves, but there may be other opportunities as well. Look for blank walls with untapped potential, and think about where extra storage would be most useful. Consider adding shelves near the tub for towels or a niche in the shower for soap and shampoo.

These built-in features not only allow you to customize storage space to fit your needs, but they also upgrade the look of your bath—especially when trimmed with molding or backed by a decorative material. Transform built-in shelves into a focal-point display space to add a touch of color and welcome personality.

A SMALL NICHE built into the wall above the tub's fixtures, *right*, provides convenient storage for bathing supplies. Teak boards pair practical water-resistance and a charming nautical look.

TWIN STORAGE TOWERS flank a freestanding tub, *far right*, creating a symmetrical tableau and providing each partner with space for grooming supplies. Hooks on either side of the tub are handy for hanging robes.

built-in storage

TEAK SHELVES, *above,* surround a stacked washer and dryer—keeping detergent and other laundry essentials close at hand and making it easy to put away just-washed towels. Folding floor-to-ceiling doors close off the laundry closet when it's not in use.

CUTE CUBBIES, *above right,* bring artistic display space to a cottage bath. Painted white and framed with molding, the cubbies pop against walls of powder blue paneling.

A SHALLOW CABINET built into the wall next to the sink, *right,* amplifies storage at this elegant vanity. Inside the cabinet, baskets keep grooming supplies organized. A stack of hand towels conveniently tucks into an open cubby below the cabinet.

RECESSED SHELVING at one end of the tub, *left,* makes smart use of space between wall studs. Trim shelves with molding for an elegant look—or add beaded-board panels at the back of shelves for charming cottage appeal.

SMALL DRAWERS, *below, far left,* tuck into the outside of the shower wall and slide underneath the bench inside the shower. They offer a creative way to supplement storage at the bath's vanity.

WALNUT CABINETS with open shelves for display, *below left,* introduce a formal, living-room style that upgrades this bath into a sophisticated retreat.

TWO NICHES built into one wall of the shower, *below,* serve as handy landing spots for soaps and shampoos. Mosaic tile backs the niches, adding texture and modern style.

lifestyle designs

Designing for the way you live and use the space offers a no-fail strategy for creating a kitchen or bath that not only looks good but feels good, too.

kitchens
120 for the serious cook
126 for the entertainer
130 for the busy family

baths
136 for the spa-lover
140 for the working couple
144 for the active retirees

for the
serious cook

A handy baking center emphasizes efficiency in this vintage-style kitchen, while a new island adds family-friendly comfort.

The scents of fresh-baked blueberry muffins and apple-walnut cake with caramel icing that waft across this Illinois kitchen are as inviting as the room's vintage look is charming. Designed for a frequent baker, who also happens to be a mom of two, the kitchen needed to be ultrafunctional and family-friendly. Kitchen designer Rebekah Zaveloff helped the homeowners reconfigure the former galley kitchen by opening up the space to an adjacent butler's pantry. "We made it one big room and doubled the kitchen's size," Zaveloff says. The layout change also allowed the homeowners to add an island—which now serves as a comfortable family hangout spot.

To create the hardworking baking zone the homeowners desired, Zaveloff located the main sink in the island rather than along the perimeter wall. "It would have been a hard sell for a lot of clients who are used to seeing the sink under the window, but they were a lot more driven by how the space was going to be used," Zaveloff says. The new setup places a generous stretch of marble countertop (perfect for rolling out dough) right next to the range. Baking supplies—including a steel-lined drawer for flour and sugar—are stored below the countertop for easy access. A pantry across the room and a hutch in the far corner offer supplemental storage for food items, pots and pans, and everyday dishes.

A NEW ISLAND features a commercial-grade stainless-steel countertop, *right*. Its dark gray finish stands out against ivory perimeter cabinets.

for the serious cook

THE PRO-STYLE RANGE offers double ovens and a large griddle for making pancakes and eggs on weekends, *right*. Rather than a typical stainless-steel model, the family opted for an enameled stove with a light green front. "It adds a little more vintage flair," kitchen designer Rebekah Zaveloff says.

INDENTATIONS IN THE COUNTERTOP next to the refrigerator, *below,* allow the homeowner to warm eggs to room temperature without worrying about them rolling off the counter.

A STEEL-LINED DRAWER filled with flour and sugar, *bottom,* is conveniently placed under the countertop in the kitchen's baking center. A sliding lid helps keep contents fresh—and keep bugs out.

PANELING AROUND THE REFRIGERATOR makes it look like a vintage icebox, *right.* Zaveloff used real vintage hardware and plain-cut oak (rather than quartersawn) for an authentic look.

for the serious cook

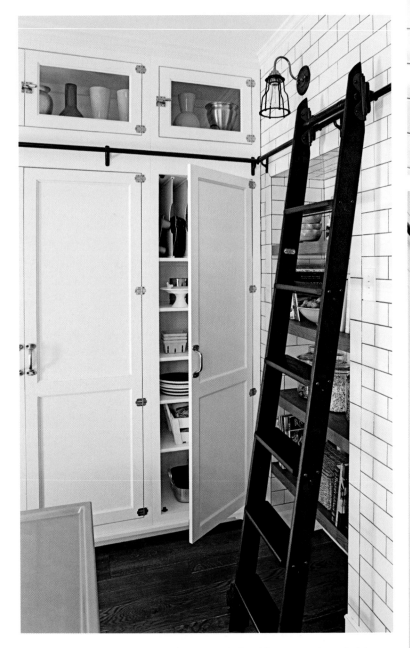

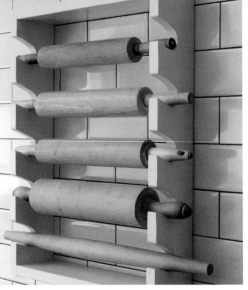

A CUSTOM ROLLING-PIN HOLDER, *left,* accents a narrow stretch of wall near the kitchen's built-in hutch—emphasizing the room's hardworking style and keeping all of the homeowner's favorite baking tools close at hand.

A PANTRY across from the range, *above,* holds food items, pots and pans, and small appliances. Vertical slots keep baking trays organized.

AN OLD DOORWAY is now outfitted with open shelves for cookbooks, *right.* A vintage library ladder offers easy access to high shelves and glass-front cabinets above the pantry.

Best Bets for Cooks

THESE CONVENIENT AMENITIES STREAMLINE MEAL PREP DUTIES.

Pro-style appliances. Choose a cooktop with high-power burners for searing meat and a simmer burner for making delicate sauces. A dual-fuel range can give you the precise control of a gas cooktop and the even baking of an electric oven.

Pot filler. If you often cook up big pots of pasta, install this special faucet near the range to decrease the need to carry heavy pots around your kitchen.

Smart spice storage. Incorporate handy pullouts or niches near the range for often-used spices and oils.

Undercabinet lighting. Add lighting under wall-mount cabinets to make cutting vegetables and reading recipes easier.

Multiple work zones. Accommodate more than one cook with separate sinks for cleanup and prep work.

THE ISLAND PREP ZONE features a sink with an integrated cutting board, *left*. The articulated-joint faucet can be folded out of the way when not in use. A hutch cabinet (background) offers attractive dish storage.

for the
entertainer

Featuring a dramatic 16-foot island, this kitchen's smart layout streamlines cooking and entertaining tasks and offers plenty of space for guests to gather.

They may be perched on one of the island's barstools or enjoying the warmth of the fire in the adjoining eating area, but guests in Bill Bocken and Paul Adams' California kitchen are always close enough to share a laugh with the cook—or even sample a bite of the dinner that's being prepared in front of them. Bill, an architect and interior designer, envisioned such scenes when he designed the open-plan kitchen around a 16-foot island that boasts a six-burner cooktop, a prep sink, refrigerator drawers, and an undercounter wine refrigerator. "It's zoned so we can do food prep and service at one end, serve drinks at the other, and let lots of people help out," Bill says.

Open storage on the kitchen's primary wall offers display space and adds welcome personality. Cabinets below the countertop are 30 inches deep (rather than the standard 24) to maximize the room's limited cabinet space. A bonus pantry on the adjacent wall offers extra storage space, tucked in discreetly next to the refrigerator, freezer, and wall ovens. Whether the dinner party is for two or 40, this kitchen's efficient floor plan and welcoming ambience put cooks and guests at ease.

AN EXTRA-DEEP SINK, *right,* helps conceal large pots during dinner parties. The faucet's sleek lines and brushed-nickel finish update the bridge-style design.

THE MARBLE-TOPPED ISLAND offers ample cooking, gathering, and storage space, *far right.* Furniture-style legs give it the look of a modern farmhouse table.

Double ovens. If you often cook for a crowd, double ovens are a must. Also consider installing a warming drawer to help you keep one dish warm while you're finishing another part of the meal.

Appliance garage. Shut the door on countertop clutter and streamline cleaning tasks before your next dinner party. Include electrical outlets inside the garage for added convenience.

Secondary dishwasher. Don't stay up late washing dishes after your next party—install a second dishwasher or a pair of dishwasher drawers to take care of all those extra plates and wineglasses.

Open floor plan. Make it easy for guests to move freely between the kitchen, dining area, and outdoor living space. Widen doorways or tear down walls to improve traffic flow. Design a kitchen layout with dedicated cooking and gathering spaces—so guests don't end up in the cook's way.

for the entertainer

ADJUSTABLE SHELVES bring a chic vibe to the cooking zone. Warm shades of gray repeat on the walls, the limestone floor, and the island top's marble veining for a unified look.

A GAS FIREPLACE at tabletop height warms a casual eating area that opens to the kitchen, *above left*. Wicker chairs and a rustic table help connect the space to the outdoors.

A PULLOUT CABINET in the island, *top*, keeps spices and oils conveniently near the cooktop.

A PAIR OF REFRIGERATOR DRAWERS, *above*, is positioned next to the island's prep sink, so the cook (or his helper) can grab fresh produce without leaving the prep space.

THE REFRIGERATOR AND FREEZER hide behind tall cabinet doors on either side of the wall ovens, *left*. A slim pantry discreetly tucks in beside open shelves in the corner.

for the
busy family

A new, open layout and a generous island help this inviting kitchen become the center of family living and entertaining.

Whether they're enjoying a casual dinner, watching television, or doing laundry, these San Francisco homeowners spend most of their time at home in the kitchen. But that wasn't always the case. The home's former layout of small, unconnected rooms left the family with no good space for casual entertaining and made it difficult to keep track of the kids while cooking. Architect David S. Gast crafted a new heart-of-the-home kitchen by opening the space to an adjoining dining room, which now serves as the family room. The new 22×12-foot kitchen is anchored by an oversize island that includes the sink and dishwasher—so the cook can easily keep an eye on kids in the family room while preparing meals or clearing dishes.

Smart amenities on both sides of the room enhance the kitchen's new multitasking role without interfering with cooking duties. On one side, a washer and dryer hide behind cabinet doors, a pantry provides supplemental storage, and a small desk offers a place for the cook to plan weekly meals. On the other side of the room, a built-in banquette overlooking the backyard serves as an inviting place for casual family meals—and makes it easy to keep an eye on kids playing outside. Finally, this family has everything they need.

A MARBLE-TOPPED ISLAND offers both prep and dining space, *right,* and subtly divides the kitchen and family room. The cabinetry's soft gray finish and glass-front doors enhance the light and airy look.

for the busy family

The kitchen welcomes family and friends with cozy seating, classic materials, and lots of natural light.

THE BUILT-IN EATING NOOK, *far left,* maximizes seating space in a small footprint; three adults can comfortably sit on each bench, and another person can pull up a chair at the end.

AN IRONING BOARD, *above left,* slides under the island countertop when not in use. It's positioned directly across the aisle from the laundry center.

A WASHER AND DRYER hide inside a cabinet with sound-dampening doors, *left.* Built-in shelves add storage space for laundry detergent and cleaning supplies.

EACH BENCH SEAT in the banquette opens up to reveal hidden storage for toys, games, and books, *below left.*

EXTRA-WIDE AISLES, *opposite,* help to accommodate two chefs, as well as two small children who like to run circles around the island. A microwave drawer and dishwasher hide on the working side of the island. The range (not shown) is directly across from the island sink, with the refrigerator just a couple of steps away; this efficient work triangle eases food preparation tasks.

LARGE-FORMAT PORCELAIN TILE above the range, *opposite,* offers a more contemporary look than traditional subway tile. A pro-style range pairs modern style and function.

A SHALLOW NICHE built into one end of the island, *top,* provides a convenient spot for cookbooks.

ROLL-OUT SHELVES, *above,* prevent items from getting lost at the back of base cabinets. Serving platters and other infrequently used items are stored on the dining side of the island.

A TALL PANTRY between the laundry center and a corner desk supplements food storage, *right.* Chrome rails on interior shelves keep contents in place but ensure they're easily accessible.

Best Bets for Family Kitchens

THESE SMART FEATURES HELP MAKE EVERYDAY TASKS EASIER.

Command center. Include a message center to help you keep track of family schedules and plan meals. This can be a built-in desk with customized storage or a corkboard and calendar installed on the back of a cabinet door.

Microwave drawer. Instead of placing the microwave above the range, install a microwave drawer that's easily accessible to all family members.

Kid-friendly storage. Consider creating a snack drawer in a base cabinet so kids can grab their own afternoon snacks or including an undercounter refrigerator for kid-friendly drinks. Hide a pullout step stool in the toe-kick under the sink cabinet to make it easier for small children to wash their hands or help with kitchen cleanup.

Lunch zone. Plan to store all your lunch-making supplies, such as sandwich bags, bread, and chips, in one area to make packing lunches quick and easy.

for the
spa-lover

Natural materials and pampering amenities
set a soothing tone in a bath that successfully brings
modern luxury to a traditional home.

When this Victorian house was built, bathrooms were simply utilitarian spaces. But the modern-day owners longed for more; they envisioned a calming retreat with spa-like luxuries and soothing colors. Architect Aleck Wilson helped them achieve their goal, borrowing square footage from an adjacent bedroom to gain space for a walk-in shower, built-in tub, dual vanity, and separate toilet compartment for added privacy. To marry the modern-day amenities with the home's traditional architecture, Wilson retained the original double-hung windows and tall ceiling and focused on timeless, natural materials. Limestone brings a muted, organic look to the floor, countertop, and tub surround, while ipe wood slats define a drying-off area beside the shower. Glass tiles in shimmering sea green tones dress up the bathroom's walls and help create the room's soothing atmosphere that allows the worries of the outside world to quietly slip away.

BUILT-IN CABINETS at one end of the vanity, *right*, offer discreet storage for everyday toiletries. Teak wood unites the custom built-ins and vanity.

SLEEK FIXTURES, streamlined hardware, and modern mosaic tile give this remodeled bath, *far right*, a clean, contemporary look. Original double-hung windows guarantee abundant natural light for grooming tasks.

for the spa-lover

ADJUSTABLE SHOWERHEADS, including a handheld fixture and a wall-mount showerhead that can be raised and lowered, enhance flexibility and convenience in the shower, *left*.

A SEPARATE TOILET ROOM, *above*, increases privacy and allows both homeowners to use the bath simultaneously. Robes and towels are within easy reach in the drying-off area outside the shower.

A FLAT-SCREEN TELEVISION nestles into a wall niche beside the whirlpool tub, *below*. The TV can be pulled away from the wall so it's visible from the vanity area as well.

THE FRAMELESS GLASS SHOWER ENCLOSURE, *opposite*, makes the shower—and the surrounding room—feel larger. A bench crafted from ipe wood offers a convenient spot to sit down and matches the wood slats outside the shower. Wall niches below the window add seamless storage.

Steam shower. You'll need a steam generator and a steamproof enclosure for this luxury feature. Don't forget to add a bench, too.

Hidden television. For the ultimate in style and convenience, install a mirror with an integrated television. Turn it on and it's a TV; turn it off and it looks like a regular mirror.

Waterfall tub filler. These models turn a utilitarian fixture into a relaxing water feature—and showcase the magnetic flow of water. Wall-mount and deck-mount tub fillers are available.

Comfortable seating. Place an upholstered chair near the tub and you suddenly have a cozy place to savor a morning cup of coffee.

Undercounter refrigerator. Tuck a small refrigerator in the corner of your bath to keep bottles of water (or wine) handy.

for the
working couple

A spacious layout with separate vanities and a roomy shower allows this bath to easily accommodate both homeowners at once.

You might say this bathroom is like two baths in one. Thanks to some creative floor-plan tweaks, interior designer Suzanne Biers found enough space to create a master bath with everything these homeowners wanted: two vanities, two walk-in closets, a shower designed for two, and two separate toilet compartments. The luxurious floor plan allows the homeowners to easily use the space at the same time—whether they're rushing to get ready on a busy morning or enjoying a relaxing evening at home. Sophisticated materials, such as glass mosaic wall tile, marble countertops, and combed porcelain floor tiles, give the bathroom a glamorous look that complements its star-studded amenities. Yet the focus on natural materials and the bath's practical layout help ground the space and ensure it's as comfortable as it is stunning.

A WALL-MOUNT FAUCET brings a modern look to the vanity sink, *right*. The faucet's matte platinum finish complements the bath's chocolate brown, white, and gray tones.

THE TWO VANITIES, featuring riftsawn oak and Carrara marble tops, are on full display as you enter the bath, *far right*. Glass mosaic tiles installed vertically emphasize the bathroom's tall ceilings.

Dual sinks. Make sure a vanity with two sinks is at least 5 feet wide to ensure comfort—or opt for separate vanities. If space is an issue, consider placing the vanities back to back or installing two pedestal sinks next to each other.

Individualized storage. Include a medicine cabinet or storage tower for each person—and organize it to fit your specific needs.

Separate toilet compartment. Giving the toilet its own room enhances privacy. Consider using a frosted-glass door to admit light but block views.

Spacious shower. Install separate showerheads, ideally on opposite walls. Consider adding a walk-through shower that offers access from both sides of the room.

for the working couple

AN EGG-SHAPE TUB doubles as sculpture, *left*. A barn-style door marks the entrance to the wife's closet, which is equipped with a washer and dryer. A television is included on the wall opposite the tub (not shown).

THE SPACIOUS STEAM SHOWER, *opposite, top left*, includes body sprays on both sides—and a handshower to make cleaning the space easier. Marble slabs featuring a water-jet-cut quatrefoil pattern lend drama to the shower walls.

A DRESSING TABLE offers a handy place for applying makeup, *opposite, top right*. It's situated on a wall adjacent to the wife's vanity; the wood door to the right leads to her water closet.

THE WIFE'S VANITY, *opposite, bottom left*, is smaller than her spouse's but is paired with a tall storage cabinet. White reverse-painted glass doors hide contents but lighten the cabinet's overall look.

A CURVED BENCH in the shower works well with the curved back wall, *opposite, bottom right*. Small mosaic tiles on the bench and shower floor add welcome pattern—and increase traction.

Eye-catching tile and distinctive finishes bring layers of texture and pattern to this inviting bath.

for the
active retirees

Elegant architectural details and luxurious materials conceal accessible design features that will allow this Michigan homeowner to stay in her home for many years to come.

The first thing you notice in this bath are the elegant marble surfaces, leaded windows and door, and decorative gold accents. But what you don't notice is equally important. Within the bathroom's luxurious framework, architect Kelly Kerlin-Ropposch and interior designer Lynn Meagher Pettyjohn added functional features that make this space work for a woman with mobility issues. She hopes to stay in the house as she ages, so the design team included wide doorways and aisles to accommodate a wheelchair in the future.

They opted for a walk-in shower and wrapped the room with a wood-profiled subcornice that elegantly disguises additional task lighting for the vanity and tub areas. Instead of slippery marble slabs for the floor, they selected 1½-inch marble tiles with more grout lines for added traction. The finished bath proved to the homeowner—and anyone who sees the bath—that high style and accessible design can go hand in hand. Instead of being reminded constantly about her limitations, she revels in the day's possibilities.

A LEADED-GLASS DOOR leading into the bath, *right*, is wide enough to accommodate a wheelchair if needed. The 36-inch-wide door repeats a scrolled design found in the transom windows throughout the home.

THE FOCAL-POINT TUB features a side-entry door for easy accessibility, *far right*. Cabinet panels around the tub match the surrounding vanity and dressing table.

EYE-CATCHING PILASTERS flank the centrally located tub and reach up toward the barrel-vault ceiling, *opposite*. Leaded-glass transoms add architectural character and admit abundant natural light.

Best Bets for Active Retirees

THESE ACCESSIBLE FEATURES ARE A SMART CHOICE FOR ANY BATH.

Barrier-free showers. These showers are flush with the adjacent floor and help prevent falls because they don't have an edge to step over. You'll need to slant the floor toward the drain—or opt for a prefabricated unit that's sized to replace an existing bathtub.

Ergonomic hardware and fixtures. Opt for faucets with lever handles, which are easy to grasp, and D-shape door and drawer pulls rather than knobs.

Stylish grab bars. Today's grab bars feature decorative finishes and smart designs; they can double as toilet paper holders, shower shelves, and towel racks. Use them throughout the bath, but especially near the entrance of the tub.

Comfort-height toilets. These taller models make it easier to sit down—and get back up.

Adequate lighting. Illuminate the bath's entry, vanity area, shower, and tub. Consider choosing a medicine cabinet or toilet seat with an integrated night-light.

for the active retirees

THE VANITY was modeled after a furniture piece the interior designer found. Gold banding and a Calacatta gold marble top elevate the look. The design team decided to optimize storage now—but doors can be removed later to accommodate a wheelchair if needed.

A WALK-IN SHOWER, *right*, features a 36-inch-wide door and is easier to step into than a tub/shower combination unit. Shower controls are positioned at an easy-to-reach height, and a grab bar offers a safeguard against falls.

Refurbished historical light fixtures and recessed lights bring classic style and modern function.

THE DRESSING TABLE, *left,* shows off delicately turned legs and inset drawers for an elegant, furniture look. The knee well is wide enough for a wheelchair, and easy-to-grasp cabinet pulls ensure the vanity's storage is accessible.

shopping guide

Find advice and buying tips about everything you'll need to purchase for your kitchen or bathroom.

cabinetry

The cabinets you choose have a big impact on the style—and cost—of your finished kitchen. Here's what you need to know to find cabinetry that's right for you.

Cabinet Basics

Kitchen cabinets are available as stock, semicustom, or custom units. Your choice will affect the overall cost and the sizes and accessories that are available.

Stock: Sold ready to install at home centers and dealers or ready to assemble online, stock cabinets are standing inventory, so you can get them quickly. Your dealer might not have every unit in stock, but special orders take as little as a week. Stock cabinetry is usually available in widths up to 48 inches, in 3-inch increments. Costs are the lowest.

Semicustom: Next up in price, semicustom cabinetry is also factory-made in standard sizes, but you'll find more woods, finishes, and decorative features. Options include pantry units, sliding shelves, and drawer inserts. These cabinetry lines generally require a longer lead time than stock cabinets.

Custom: With the most options to offer, custom cabinetry, *right,* is designed, built, and installed to fit your space. A professional kitchen designer will help establish an efficient layout. Exotic woods, ornate details, and period styles will add cost and delivery time but result in a one-of-a-kind kitchen.

Cabinet Construction

Your cabinetry's construction style affects your kitchen's look and the available storage space.

1. FACE FRAME In this traditional-look construction, a solid-wood frame attaches to the front of the cabinet box. Hinges, hidden or visible, attach the door to the frame. Because the frame overlaps the door opening, drawers must be slightly narrower than the cabinet box. If you would like to add decorative accessories, such as corbels and fluted stiles, this option is a good choice.

2. FRAMELESS This more contemporary-look construction features doors that attach directly to the cabinet boxes. These cabinets eliminate space-stealing frames and offer slightly more capacity. Door hinges mount inside the cabinet, so they're hidden when doors are closed. If you want to maximize storage space, this option is for you.

MONEY-WISE

Are your cabinets in good shape but no longer in style? Save thousands of dollars on your kitchen remodel by refacing your cabinets instead of replacing them. Order new drawer and door fronts, then add matching self-stick veneer to the face frame. This technique works well for partial-overlay doors, but it can also be used for full-overlay and inset doors if you measure cabinets carefully.

cabinetry

Style Details

The door style and material you choose for your kitchen cabinetry can help you achieve your desired look. Slab doors are flat and sleek—ideal for a contemporary space. Paneled doors range from simple mitered squares to gentle arches or fancier cathedral tops and can complement a range of decorating styles. Glass-front cabinets with decorative mullions, *right,* can lighten your kitchen's overall look and add charming detail.

Natural wood offers a selection of colors and grains. Oak, pine, and hickory boast prominent grain patterns and suit traditional or country styles. Maple, cherry, and mahogany look classic or contemporary, depending on the finish. Stain affects wood color and shows its grain, while paint creates a solid finish that hides grain. Glazes add depth and give new cabinets an old-fashioned look.

Laminate, melamine (a durable plastic), or **heat-set vinyl** (called thermofoil) wipe clean easily and resist chipping. They are often used on more contemporary cabinetry.

Door and Drawer Design

Full Overlay: Doors cover the face frame—or the entire box front on frameless cabinets—leaving minimal space between doors and drawers, *right.*

Partial Overlay: Doors cover the frame by about ½ inch; the rest of the frame shows around the door. This type of door might slightly reduce your cabinetry cost; the door is smaller so less material is used, *middle right.*

Inset: Doors and drawer fronts install flush with the face frame, *far right,* resulting in a narrower drawer. The precision of this design is most often seen in custom cabinetry.

Cabinet Hardware

Whether you're replacing your cabinets or keeping the old ones, new cabinet hardware, *right,* can give your kitchen a whole new look. Choose knobs and pulls with brushed finishes for a traditional look, old-fashioned bin pulls for a vintage style, or sleek stainless-steel pulls to add a touch of modern flair to your cooking zone. Consider ergonomics as well as finish and style when selecting new hardware; drawer pulls large enough to grasp with the whole hand are the easiest to use.

Cabinet Interior Hardware

To make the most of every inch of storage space, shop for interior hardware options that make contents easy to organize and access. Some basic storage accessories are available in stock cabinetry lines, but you'll find more options in semicustom and custom cabinets.

Interior storage accessories will add to your overall cabinet cost, but they can greatly improve the functionality of your cooking zone. Consider storing cookware on pullout shelves or wire organizers, for example, or add spice pullouts near the range. Angled corner drawers or special corner cabinets with a lazy Susan or pullout shelves put potentially wasted space to work. Pullout pantries, *right,* add hardworking storage for canned and dry goods within the primary cooking zone.

If you're not replacing your cabinetry but want to upgrade your storage, consider the retrofitted options available at home centers. Tiered pullout baskets, drawer organizers, and under-the-sink organizers can be added to existing cabinetry to enhance available storage space and keep items organized.

Design Tips
SMART CABINETRY CHOICES CAN UPGRADE YOUR KITCHEN'S STYLE.

Mix it up. Vary the cabinet finish or door style to give your kitchen a remodeled-over-time feel. Consider setting off the island with a contrasting finish.

Conceal appliances. Give your kitchen a living-room style by hiding appliances behind panels that match surrounding cabinetry.

Create a focal point. Hide the range hood with custom cabinetry that mimics the look of an old-fashioned hearth.

Provide visual relief. Resist the urge to cover every inch of wall space with cabinetry. Large windows, open shelves, or eye-catching tile work enhance a kitchen's overall look and feel.

ranges, ovens & cooktops

Modern cooking appliances offer convenient features that help streamline meal preparation tasks. Here's what to look for when you shop for ranges, ovens, and cooktops.

Whether you opt for an all-in-one range or a separate cooktop and wall oven, new appliances can help you prepare food faster and customize your cooking experience.

Ranges

Most traditional ranges—with four burners on top and an oven below—are 30 inches wide, but 24- and 36-inch models are also available. Commercial-style models are 48 or 60 inches wide to accommodate six burners or a combination of burners and a griddle or grill, *right*. Some models boast two ovens or a built-in warming drawer. Bakers often prefer the even heat of electricity, which has led to the introduction of dual-fuel models that pair an electric oven with gas burners on top. Ranges can be freestanding (with finished side panels) or made to slide between cabinets. Typically, purchasing a range is less expensive than a separate cooktop and oven.

Ovens

Built into a wall or under a counter, 30- or 36-inch-wide ovens offer thermal or convection (or combination) cooking in single or double cavities. Convection models use a fan to circulate air for faster and more even baking. Built-in, speed-cook ovens typically combine thermal, convection, and microwave functions for added convenience—but usually come with a higher price tag. Some ovens combine steam and convection; steam helps food stay moist and preserves valuable nutrients. If you often cook meals for large gatherings, choose an oven with a large capacity, or opt for two ovens or a range with an additional wall oven.

Cooktops

You can choose among three types of cooktops, based on your cooking preferences and needs.

1. GAS Traditionally, gas cooktops have been the choice of serious cooks, thanks to their fast heat and instant control. To ease cleaning tasks, opt for sealed burners that prevent liquid and food debris from getting below the cooktop. Continuous grates make it easy to slide pots from one burner to another. Pilotless ignition is standard, and some cooktops also offer reigniting burners, which automatically relight if the flame goes out. Look for burners with various BTU levels to more easily sear foods and simmer delicate sauces.

2. ELECTRIC Most electric cooktops are smooth-top models; their sleek surface makes it easy to wipe up spills, although they do require a special cleaner. Electric cooktops now offer rapid-cycle elements that fine-tune the heat setting as precisely as gas. Look for models with expandable elements that feature a small, low-power element within a larger, high-power element, or bridge elements that accommodate oversize cookware or a griddle. Opt for models with indicator lights that tell you which burners are turned on or still hot.

3. INDUCTION These cooktops generate a magnetic field that heats the pan but not the cooktop surface—making them a safe choice for families with small children. Induction cooktops are more expensive than many gas or electric options, but the elements heat up quickly and are very energy-efficient. With a smooth ceramic glass top, they're also easy to clean. They do, however, require magnetic cookware. (If a magnet sticks to the bottom of a pan, it will work on the cooktop.)

microwave ovens

Cook food fast and enhance convenience with these savvy cooking appliances. Take a look at the different types of models available—and the features you should look for when shopping.

Before you purchase a microwave oven, you need to know where you plan to install it. Think about what placement will work best for your family (and your kitchen's layout), and choose a model accordingly.

Countertop

Available in a range of sizes and oven capacities, these models have features similar to a built-in model but take up space on the countertop. Many are sold with trim kits so they can be built into cabinetry if desired.

Built-In

Designed to be surrounded by cabinetry, these units sometimes feature a drop-down door similar to traditional ovens. Often these models are installed above or below a wall oven. For a unified look, you can choose a trim kit that matches your other appliances, *right*.

Over-the-Range

These models combine a microwave oven and a ventilation fan and are installed above your range or cooktop. This arrangement might place the microwave oven too high for short cooks; reaching over a hot range or cooktop to access it raises safety concerns for all users. Although the ventilation is strong enough for many residential kitchens, it's not powerful enough for pro-style ranges and cooktops. It's useful when space is at a premium.

Drawer

Drawer-style microwave ovens can be installed below a countertop or paired with a wall oven. They're ideal for kitchens with limited counter space or for island configurations. They slide open just like a drawer and can be placed at a height that's convenient for all family members. They are pricier than countertop models and have limited installation options.

Smart Features

THESE OPTIONS SIMPLIFY COOKING.

Speed-cook models. Featuring microwave and convection technology, they cook food fast and evenly. They can operate like a second oven because they can also be used for baking and browning.

Programmed settings. Look for buttons for popcorn, baked potatoes, pizza, and more.

Smart sensors. These automatically turn the oven off when food is done.

Easy-clean features. A removable turntable, grease filters, and a nonstick interior ease cleanup.

Warming lamp. This helps keep food warm after it's finished cooking.

range hoods

Whisk away smoke and odors with a new ventilation system that matches or exceeds your cooktop's requirements. Here's what you need to know before choosing a model.

Vent Fan Capacity

Vent fan capacity is rated by how many cubic feet of air per minute (cfm) a fan removes. If you use the vent fan once or twice a day and cook on a conventional electric range, you need a fan rated at 160–200 cfm. For similar use with a conventional gas range, choose a vent fan with a capacity of 200–300 cfm. If you do lots of cooking on a professional- or semiprofessional-style gas range, you'll need as much as 1,500 cfm.

Fan Sound Level

The sound level is measured in sones. Lower numbers designate quieter units. One sone, for example, is similar to the sound of a quiet refrigerator in a quiet room. Doubling the sone rating is the same as doubling the sound level of the appliance.

Hood Width

The width of the ventilation hood should never be less than the width of the cooking surface. In most cases, it should be wider than the cooking surface to help trap more smoke, grease, and odors.

Mounting Height

It's crucial that your ventilation hood be the proper distance above your cooking surface. The recommended installation height for conventional hoods is usually 18–24 inches above the cooking surface and 24–30 inches for high-performance hoods. Refer to the installation manuals for your hood and your cooktop or range for specific instructions.

Design Options

Several different types of range hoods are available to fit your installation needs.

Undercabinet: These hoods work well with ranges or cooktops that produce few BTUs. They mount to the wall or to the bottom of a wall cabinet, through which ductwork can be routed outside.

Chimney Hoods: These models work where there are no cabinets directly above the range or cooktop, *top right.* They mount with a decorative cover that hides the ductwork, offering a stylish focal point in a kitchen.

Island Hoods: As their name implies, these models are used above islands, *middle right;* they're mounted to the ceiling and vented through ductwork above. An island hood should be wider than the cooktop—ideally by 3 inches on both sides.

Custom Inserts: A custom insert offers unlimited design choices. The guts of the ventilation are hidden in a surround, so these inserts can be hidden in cabinetry that matches the rest of your kitchen.

Downdrafts: These ventilation fans, *bottom right,* draw out air through ductwork under the floor. Downdraft ventilation offers space efficiency and a sleek look; they can be a good choice in kitchens with a cathedral ceiling or where a traditional hood would block the view.

refrigerators & freezers

A variety of design styles and interior options make it easy to find a refrigerator that suits your family's storage needs and complements the way you work in the kitchen.

Today's refrigerators are designed to maximize organization and connectivity. Models with LCD screens and apps on the front, for example, allow you to listen to music, check the weather, make grocery lists, or find out the latest news. Fingerprint-resistant door finishes can help ease cleaning chores. Inside the refrigerator, flexible storage options can help make your life easier. Look for removable condiment caddies, customizable dividers, and adjustable door bins and shelves. Some models include features to help moderate temperature and humidity to keep food fresh longer. Thanks to more efficient compressors and better insulation, new refrigerators are more energy efficient than older models.

Refrigerators are available as either freestanding, counter-depth, or built-in units—and in a variety of configurations. Here's what you need to know when shopping:

Refrigerator Type
Freestanding: Standard refrigerators measure 27–32 inches deep, so they stand out from standard 24-inch-deep base cabinets. They're available in four configurations: top-freezer, bottom-freezer, side-by-side, or French door. They're less expensive than built-in models and offer the most usable storage space, but they make it more difficult to achieve a custom, built-in look.

Counter-Depth: Get the upscale look of a built-in for less money with a counter-depth refrigerator. These models extend just a little past surrounding countertops to allow space for the doors to swing open. Most are side-by-side models, but bottom-freezers and French door models are also available.

Built-In: More expensive than freestanding units, these 24-inch-deep models fit flush with cabinets, *opposite,* and can match surrounding cabinetry when outfitted with custom front panels. They're generally available in bottom-freezer and side-by-side configurations. Full-size all-freezer and all-refrigerator units are another built-in variation for a custom kitchen. Because built-ins are wide but relatively shallow, they're not the most space-efficient option.

Configurations
Top-Freezer: A budget-friendly option, this configuration places the frozen-food compartment at eye level and the fresh-food compartment below.

Bottom-Freezer: This configuration places the freezer below the fresh-food compartment, so the often-accessed fresh food is at a user-friendly height.

Side-by-Side: These units are split vertically, with frozen food on the left and fresh food on the right. When open, the slender doors occupy less floor space, so they can be an advantage in small kitchens, but the doors can block countertop access on both sides. Narrow compartments make bulky items difficult to store, and food items tend to get lost in the back of the refrigerator.

French Door: These armoire-style models store fresh food behind twin doors at eye level and frozen food in a drawer below. Pullout baskets in the freezer compartment enhance convenience, and wide door openings make it easier to store bulky items.

Undercounter: These refrigerators slide under the countertop (most at counter depth) and are ideal for storing snacks and beverages outside the main work triangle or produce near the prep sink. High-end wine refrigerators offer multitemperature storage zones as well as pullout shelves that are tilted to help keep corks moist.

Drawer: Refrigerator and freezer drawers install under a counter, in a wall, or in an island. They're ideal for storing fresh produce near the prep sink, afternoon snacks for kids, or drinks for guests. Because drawers don't offer much capacity, they are commonly used in addition to a full-size refrigerator.

Smart Features

LOOK FOR OPTIONS THAT INCREASE VERSATILITY.

Adjustable door bins and shelves. Some models feature elevator shelves, which allow you to raise or lower them easily—without removing all the food. Split shelves also increase flexibility.

Through-the-door ice and water dispenser. Included in most side-by-side models, this feature enhances convenience but uses more energy and often needs to be repaired.

Door alarms. These alarms alert you if the door has been left open.

Spill-proof glass shelves. Featuring raised edges, these shelves capture spills so they don't leak onto lower shelves.

Freshness features. Look for sensor-based temperature and humidity-regulation systems and crisper drawers that help keep food fresh longer.

kitchen sinks

Create a smart and stylish cleanup zone with a kitchen sink that complements your work style and dresses up your cooking area with sleek style or old-fashioned charm.

Sink Materials

Cast Iron: Featuring a layer of porcelain enamel over cast iron, these sinks are durable and easy to maintain. Sinks are heavy, though, and apron-front models, *above,* often require special sink-base cabinets.

Cast Acrylic: Made of plastic that is reinforced with fiberglass, these sinks are lightweight, easy to install, and affordable. Their surface is stain-resistant.

Composite: Made of a mixture of materials, these lightweight sinks feature a durable, low-maintenance surface and are available in a variety of colors. Molded-through color helps hide chips and scratches.

Copper: These sinks will acquire an aged patina over time. They're good for prep areas because the metal helps kill bacteria.

Fireclay: These sinks have been fired at very high temperatures, resulting in a durable surface that's resistant to ships, stains, scratches, and bacteria.

Stainless Steel: These sinks are affordable, durable, and easy to clean. But be sure to check the gauge: The lower the gauge, the thicker the metal—and the more durable and quieter the sink when pots clang against it. Brushed and satin stainless steel help hide scratches, water spots, and fingerprints.

Stone: Featuring a stylish, organic look, these sinks are costly to buy and install. The surface is unforgiving of dropped plates and glasses.

Sink Configurations

Single-Bowl: These sinks offer ample space for washing large pans and baking sheets.

Double-Bowl: Available with two bowls of equal size or one larger bowl and one smaller bowl, these sinks let you multitask more easily.

Three-Bowl: With extra options in depth and proportion, this sink style has a third, shallow bowl for food prep.

Modular: This sink has individual bowls that come in several shapes and sizes. You create your ideal arrangement.

Bar/Prep: Ideal for entertaining areas or island work centers, these smaller, secondary sinks come in a variety of geometric shapes.

Sink Installation

Drop-In: Also called top-mount or self-rimming, these sinks are easy to install and affordable. They feature a lip that overlaps the countertop, which can be difficult to clean. They can be used with any type of countertop.

Undermount: These sinks are installed under the countertop, so there's no lip to catch food and dirt. They offer a seamless look, but they are typically more expensive and harder to install than drop-in models.

Apron-Front: Also called farmhouse sinks, these models feature an exposed front that makes them a design focal point. They add vintage charm, but they're often pricey— and water can drip down their exposed front and potentially damage cabinets below.

PLANNING TIP

Be sure to consider how many faucet holes you'll need in your kitchen sink. A single-handle faucet requires one hole, while faucets with separate hot and cold handles require three. Add another hole if you want a sidespray, hot water dispenser, or built-in soap dispenser.

kitchen faucets

Pairing eye-catching finishes with smart function, today's faucets ease prep and cleanup tasks. A range of available styles ensures your faucet can complement your kitchen's design.

Showing off sleek, contemporary designs or vintage elegance, faucets help set the tone of your cooking and cleanup areas and can bring welcome drama to a simple sink. Popular options, such as pullout faucets, and newer technologies, such as hands-free faucets, increase convenience in busy kitchen work areas, while low-flow models conserve water. Here's a look at the various faucet styles available and the benefits of each type.

Faucet Styles

1. BRIDGE FAUCET An exposed channel links handles and spout in this classic faucet style that complements traditional-style kitchens.

2. COMMERCIAL-STYLE Adapted from restaurant kitchens, this faucet type boasts a tall, flexible spray hose that reaches any sink corner.

3. GOOSENECK OR HIGH-ARC This tall, arched spout makes it easy to fill deep pots and tall vases.

4. POT FILLER Mounted on a wall near a range or cooktop, this faucet makes filling pots easy.

5. PULLOUT OR PULL-DOWN FAUCET A two-piece spout functions as both a faucet and a retractable sprayer.

6. SINGLE-HOLE Only one hole pierces the sink deck or countertop, conserving space.

7. WALL-MOUNT These space-savvy faucets are plumbed through the wall behind the sink.

PLANNING TIP

For extra convenience, try a hands-free faucet. An electronic sensor turns these faucets on when you place your hands below the tap. Touch faucets are also available, which turn on and off with the light touch of a hand or arm to any part of the faucet.

dishwashers

Enhance convenience in your cleanup zone with a dishwasher that pairs convenient features and a streamlined look. Here's what to look for when you're shopping for a new model.

Most dishwashers fit into a 24-inch-wide space under the kitchen countertop, but the interior options can vary greatly by price. Budget-priced models clean dishes well but offer fewer options, such as flexible loading features, *right,* and tend to be noisier than upscale models. New dishwashers use less water and energy, and many include a range of special wash features to allow you to customize your settings for specific needs. The three basic settings—light, normal, and heavy (pots and pans)—should be enough for most chores, however. To minimize noise, look for models with extra insulation, cushioned tubs, and special motors that reduce water use and mechanical noise. Cabinet panels (available as kits from most dishwasher manufacturers) can disguise the dishwasher and provide a seamless look. Consider whether you want electronic controls integrated into the top edge of the door to further streamline the look, or a front-facing control panel that allow you to see where the dishwasher is in its cycle.

Dishwasher drawers offer an alternative to traditional dishwashers. Typically, these feature two stacked drawers that can be used together or individually. Their pullout drawers make loading and unloading easy, and they efficiently handle small loads. They can be a good choice for small households or as an extra dishwasher for larger households. They are typically more expensive than standard-size dishwashers, however.

PLANNING TIP
When arranging appliances, be sure to physically separate the dishwasher and refrigerator. The dishwasher produces heat and will increase the energy consumption of your refrigerator.

Smart Features
THESE OPTIONS BOOST EFFICIENCY AND CONVENIENCE.

Adjustable racks. These let you configure the interior for specific items.

A built-in disposer. This feature breaks up and traps large food particles, eliminating the need to prerinse. Some models have a filter without a grinder—a quieter option.

Delayed start. Wash dishes when it's convenient—or when water rates are low.

No-heat drying. This feature saves energy but also increases drying time.

Sensors. They detect the amount of soil in the water and adjust water use and cycle length accordingly.

kitchen lighting

A good lighting plan will help create a safe and inviting room. Think about light fixtures early in the remodeling process to ensure you can add light where you really need it.

The kitchen is at the center of many types of activities, so it deserves a complex lighting plan that addresses the room's various roles. Good overall lighting ensures the kitchen is a welcoming place for friends and family to gather, but you'll also want efficient light aimed at kitchen work areas.

Task Lighting
Be sure to illuminate work surfaces in the main cooking and prep spaces. Undercabinet lighting can be an excellent option here; many low-profile fixtures can easily be hidden from view. Affordable xenon lights are cooler than halogen bulbs and can easily be retrofitted into an existing kitchen. Choose from strips or puck lights. Track lighting and pendant lights above an island, *right,* are also popular ways to add efficient task lighting at the center of the room. The basic rule for the height of a pendant light is 35–40 inches above the work surface. Also consider adding a light fixture over the primary sink to illuminate the cleanup zone.

Ambient Lighting
This type of lighting provides general illumination for the room and substitutes for natural lighting when it's not available. Recessed ceiling lights arranged around the room are especially useful when the kitchen is being used simultaneously by several people for different purposes such as cooking, homework, and socializing. A surface-mount ceiling light in the center of the room can also work—or opt for a chandelier for a touch of drama. You can add a gentle glow around the

perimeter of the room with cove lighting. In this scenario, rope lights are hidden behind a molding installed several inches below the ceiling. Consider installing dimmers so you can save energy and change the mood when entertaining.

Accent Lighting
Add a special spotlight or aim track lights so they illuminate a prized collection of dishware or pottery, a dramatic piece of artwork, or a striking architectural feature.

Design Tips
CONSIDER THESE FACTORS WHEN CHOOSING LIGHTBULBS AND FIXTURES.

Bulb type. Compact fluorescent lamps (CFLs) are small fluorescent bulbs that offer up to eight years of life. They emit light in all directions but take time to brighten. Light-emitting diode bulbs (LEDs) brighten instantly and can last up to five times longer—making them a great choice for hard-to-reach fixtures.

Color temperature. The type and shade of light is measured in a temperature rating known as Kelvin (K). Higher Kelvin temperatures produce a bluer light that's similar to natural sunlight; this color of light can work well in kitchen work areas.

Color rendering. The color rendering index, or CRI, tells you how accurately colors appear under the bulb's light. The index ranges from 0 to 100, with 100 equal to daytime sunlight. You'll likely want a CRI of at least 80 for most interior light fixtures.

countertops & wall surfaces

Smart and stylish surfaces bring welcome color and pattern to kitchens and baths. Mix multiple materials to add visual interest and highlight specific areas of the room.

Countertop Materials

Bamboo: This renewable grass offers an eco-friendly countertop option. Make sure it's assembled using food-safe adhesives if you plan to use it in the kitchen. Water can warp the material, so it's best in lesser-used areas.

Butcher Block: Made from laminated wood, this works well for baking areas and island tops. Seal with oil to boost moisture-resistance; let knife marks create a patina, or sand the surface smooth.

Concrete: Cast in place or installed as preformed slabs, sealed concrete resists burns, stains, and scratches but is labor-intensive to install. Customize it with tints, texture, inset shells or glass, or other items.

Cultured Marble: Sold in sheet form and standard counter depths, this material is made of natural marble chips embedded in plastic resin. Less pricey than real marble, it can be used for bathroom countertops and walls.

Glass: Sleek and dramatic, tempered glass comes in clear or translucent forms with a smooth or textured surface. Recycled composite glass is also an option. Glass is waterproof and heat-tolerant. Use a cutting board in the kitchen to avoid scratches.

Granite: This popular stone offers a variety of colors and patterns. Shopping at a stoneyard costs more than ordering from a sample but lets you buy the exact piece you want. Reduce cost by using granite tiles or remnants instead of a single slab. Granite is durable and impervious to heat but requires professional installation and periodic sealing.

Laminate: Affordable laminate comes preformed as a one-piece counter and backsplash in limited color choices. Or if you custom-order from a home center or kitchen dealer, you'll find hundreds of colors and patterns, some that mimic stone, metal, or wood. The material is easy to install but typically has visible seams on the front edge unless you add a decorative edge. Use a cutting board for slicing and trivets for hot pans, as laminate can't be repaired.

Marble and Limestone: These stones are classic and luxurious, but they're softer and more porous than granite so they're more likely to scratch or stain. Marble is ideal for rolling out dough in a baking area or for adding an upscale look to a bath.

Quartz-Surfacing: Also called engineered stone, this blend of ground quartz, resins, and pigments produces consistent stonelike patterns. It is nonporous and heat- and scratch-resistant.

Soapstone: Soft and silky, soapstone chips more easily than granite but provides a classic look that complements traditional decors. Like other stones, it resists heat. You'll need to treat it with mineral oil periodically to help repel moisture and keep it looking nice.

Solid-Surfacing: Look for panels and veneers made of plastic resins in many colors and patterns. The nonporous material resists stains; scratches can be sanded out. Solid-surfacing sinks create a seamless installation.

Stainless Steel: Sanitary and stainproof, this surface complements a stainless-steel sink and perfects a pro-style kitchen. Steel is heatproof and waterproof, but a shiny finish can show scratches and fingerprints. Ready-made sections fit standard counter sizes; custom installations fit others.

Tile: Glazed ceramic or porcelain tiles in many shapes, colors, and sizes are water- and heat-resistant. Many tiles are inexpensive, and if they chip, they're easy to replace. You might need to regrout tile countertops every few years; darker grout can help hide stains.

Wall Treatments

Tile: Ceramic, porcelain, and glass tiles are all offered in a wide range of colors and designs that can enhance your kitchen or bath. Mixing accent tiles and field tiles can help you create a custom look. Both large-format and mosaic tiles can make a bath feel larger; install tiles vertically, *above,* to make the room feel taller. Mosaics in glass, stone, and metal can be a DIY project if bought on a mesh backing. For durability, be sure to use only wall tile for walls and floor tile for floors.

Stone: Available in both tile and slab form, natural stone can bring organic beauty—and dramatic vein patterns—to bathroom walls or a kitchen backsplash. Slabs are more expensive but offer a more seamless look.

Paint: Paint is the least expensive wall treatment option. Gloss and semigloss finishes work best in the bath's humid environment, but keep in mind that they'll accentuate any irregularities on the walls. Use epoxy paint if you want to cover a tile, glass, or porcelain surface.

Wallcoverings: Use wallpaper to add personality to kitchens and baths. Vinyl coverings (especially vinyl laminated to fabric) will hold up better than traditional wallpaper in humid environments.

kitchen & bath flooring

Choose a flooring material that's comfortable and stylish in kitchen work zones where you'll be doing a lot of standing. Consider slip-resistance when choosing a floor for the shower.

A variety of flooring materials is available for the kitchen and bath—so you're sure to find one that works well in your space and suits your style and budget. Before heading to the store, take a moment to consider how much traffic the floor will get, whether it will be used in a wet area, and how much sunlight will hit the floor. The answers to these questions will help guide you to a flooring product that will work best for your intended application. Here's a look at the most popular options on the market and smart features to consider.

Bamboo

This renewable grass offers the look of wood. If you're looking for an eco-friendly option, make sure the factory finish is formaldehyde-free. Bamboo flooring is either solid or engineered; opt for engineered versions in wet environments such as bathrooms.

Cork

Made from the bark of cork oak trees, this eco-friendly option is quiet and soft underfoot. It's also fire-resistant and antimicrobial. If it's properly sealed, it can withstand moisture.

Laminate

This budget-friendly flooring choice can be a convincing, easy-care substitute for wood, tile, or stone. It's available in planks or tiles and is one of the easiest flooring types to install yourself. Good-quality laminates resist discoloration and scratches, but unlike wood floors, they can't be refinished when the outer layer wears away. Embossed and hand-scraped textures add depth and better imitate natural materials for a realistic look.

Linoleum

Made from linseed oil, cork dust, wood flour, tree resins, ground limestone, and pigments, this option is eco-friendly and soft underfoot. It's available in a variety of colors and styles, but it can be somewhat expensive.

Stone

This natural material is available in both slab and tile form. It adds upscale charm to a kitchen or bath, but it can be slippery when wet and hard underfoot. It also can require professional installation. A stone's porosity—the amount and size of its pores—affects its strength and stain-resistance. For lower maintenance in a high-traffic kitchen, choose a hard stone with low porosity, such as granite or slate. Softer, more porous stone materials, such as marble, limestone, and travertine, require regular sealing to reduce staining and scratching.

Tile

A classic choice for kitchens or baths, tile comes in a variety of shapes and sizes that can provide an opportunity for customization. Ceramic tiles resist moisture and scratches, but tiles can crack and the grout is easily stained. Porcelain tiles are dense and very durable; their scratch-resistant surface withstands spills and pet accidents. Tile is harder underfoot than some other flooring types, so glasses and dishes break more easily when dropped on a tile surface. Tile can also be slippery; if you're using tile in the shower, opt for mosaic tile rather than large-format tile for better traction.

Vinyl

Available in sheets, tiles, and planks, vinyl flooring shows off a variety of looks, including wood and stone, but is more affordable. Keep in mind, though, that higher-end vinyl does a good job of imitating natural surfaces and can be as expensive as the real thing. Vinyl is soft underfoot, durable, and moisture-resistant. Chose vinyl with a thick urethane top coat for maximum durability.

Wood

This flooring type offers a classic look that works in a variety of decorating styles. Solid wood is one continuous piece of wood from top to bottom, so it offers a thick material for sanding and refinishing, but it's susceptible to moisture. Engineered wood has a thin top layer of hardwood secured to a sturdy plywoodlike base layer. It's less expensive than solid wood and is less likely to be affected by humidity. You can buy wood unfinished or with a factory finish already applied. Unfinished wood is less expensive, but remember you'll have to hire someone to apply a finish to protect it against moisture (or do this yourself). The factory finish is likely to last longer and usually comes with a warranty.

Design Tips
ADD INTEREST UNDERFOOT WITH SMART STRATEGIES.

Add pattern. Use two different colors of tile to create a vintage checkerboard treatment or craft a unique design of your own, *left.*

Celebrate texture. Terrazzo tiles, *below right,* feature bits of natural stone and recycled glass for subtle pattern and color. Or opt for a hand-scraped wood (or laminate look-alike) that adds instant age and character.

Accent a specific feature. Install a band of mosaic tile around an island or a freestanding bathtub to create a dramatic focal point.

Consider transitions. Install transition strips or border tiles to unify two disparate flooring materials, such as tile and wood, *below left.*

PLANNING TIP
Install radiant-heat panels or mats below tile, vinyl, and hardwood floors to keep feet warm on cold winter days. Electric versions can operate on timers and warm defined areas, such as in front of the bathroom vanity, tub, or shower.

vanities, cabinets & storage

Elegant bath cabinetry upgrades the look of your bath—and adds versatile storage space. Here's what to think about before purchasing a vanity or designing cabinets for your bath.

Cabinet Basics

Like kitchen units, ready-made bath cabinets come in two basic constructions. American-style framed cabinets have a face frame applied to the front of the cabinet boxes. Door hinges are often visible. European, or frameless, cabinets have no face frame. Doors cover almost all of each cabinet box, and hardware is hidden when the doors are closed. The former suggests a traditional look; the latter usually feels more contemporary.

Stock cabinets offer the fewest variables in materials, finishes, sizes, and details, but they're also the most affordable.

Semicustom and custom cabinets increase your options—but also your cost, and typically your delivery time.

Vanity Construction

When you're shopping for bathroom vanities and cabinets, remember that you typically get what you pay for. Quality materials, such as plywood cabinet boxes and drawers with solid-wood sides and dovetail joinery, are more expensive than some other materials, but they're likely to hold up longer. You'll also need to decide if you want a vanity with a top. A vanity with a countertop simplifies your choices, but one without a top lets you pick from a wide range of countertop materials.

Style Details

Exotic woods, specialty finishes, and milled details can bring a furniture look to the vanity area and upgrade your bath's overall style. Choose a model with a bowed front, *opposite,* for an extra dash of style, or add custom moldings or pilasters to upgrade the look. Remember the decorative impact of knobs and pulls, as well. Use this cabinet jewelry to dress up a simple style or emphasize a design theme. Match your faucet finish or not—it's up to you.

Storage Features

When selecting a vanity, consider how you'll use it. What will be stored there? Do you want a single sink or a double vanity that offers more storage space? Most vanities combine drawer and shelf space, but semicustom and custom units include more customizable features, such as pullout shelves, roll-out hampers, and built-in bins for hair dryers and curling irons. Increase the versatility of stock models with retrofitted wire shelves, a pullout wastebasket, towel rods, hooks, and interior drawer dividers.

Medicine cabinets also boost storage space in the vanity area. Look for cabinets with adjustable shelves, built-in electrical outlets, and a mirror defogger (if you can afford a splurge). Use cosmetic organizers to keep small items tidy. If you're remodeling, you may want to choose the same type of medicine cabinet that you're replacing (a surface-mount or recessed unit) to avoid breaking into the wall.

DIY TIP
Shop thrift stores or recycle furniture from other rooms to create one-of-a-kind bath storage. Convert a dresser into a custom vanity or add vintage shelves for displaying collectibles. Remember to apply a moisture-resistant sealer to prevent wood from warping.

Design Tips
PLAN CAREFULLY TO PICK A VANITY THAT WORKS IN YOUR SPACE.

Measure your room. Before selecting a vanity, measure your space to ensure it will work with existing plumbing lines—or plan to pay more to move them. Also be sure to leave clearance space so you can open cabinet doors.

Consider height. Vanity cabinets usually range in height from 31 to 35 1/2 inches. If you're tall, you may want to opt for a taller vanity to reduce bending. Or choose a shorter vanity for a child's bathroom.

Enhance space. If you have a small bath, think about installing a wall-mount vanity. The open area below creates the illusion of extra space.

bathroom sinks

Create an eye-catching focal point with elegant sinks that are both stylish and functional—or let your sink blend into the surrounding countertop for a sleek and seamless look.

When choosing a sink for your bathroom, consider available space as well as the room's overall design. Here's a look at the most common types of sinks available today.

Vanity-Top

Vanity-top sinks are among the most budget-friendly. Round, oval, or square bowls of porcelain, glass, ceramic, or metal can be installed in three ways:

Drop-in, or self-rimming, sinks simply drop into a hole slightly smaller than the sink's rim and rest on the countertop surface. The slight raised rim helps capture splashes.

Undermount sinks attach below the counter surface, which is usually made of stone, engineered quartz, or solid-surfacing material. The sink's edges—and those of the surrounding countertop—must be finished perfectly for a tidy look and easy cleanup.

Integral sinks are made from the same material as the countertop. Professional installers finish the seam to be invisible.

SINK MATERIALS

Vitreous china is inexpensive and cleans easily, but it can chip. Stone and porcelain-enameled cast iron are durable but heavy. Fiberglass-reinforced plastic is lightweight, but it can show wear. Cast polymer and cultured marble may chip. Brushed or satin-finish stainless steel hides water spots. Glass must be tempered for safety.

Console

Console sinks merge the function of a vanity with furniture styling, *top right.* Wood or metal legs form an airy base for the bowl and leave plumping pipes exposed

Pedestal

Pedestal sinks, *middle right,* bring vintage character to the bathroom. These sinks occupy less space than boxy vanities but offer less storage. Choose a model with a wide deck or a towel rail to amplify storage space.

Above-Counter or Vessel Sinks

These sinks bring a sculptural presence to the vanity area and are available in many shapes and materials. The raised bowls can mean less bending and greater comfort for adults but may be difficult to use for children or people with disabilities. With the outside of the bowl exposed, you have more surface area to clean. If you opt for an above-counter sink, you may need a shorter vanity or console and a taller or wall-mount faucet. As a compromise, recess the sink partially so only some of its exterior shows above the countertop.

Wall-Mount

Wall-mount sinks, *bottom right,* are a boon to cramped quarters because the open space below the sink provides an airy look. They can be installed at any height; the open area below the sink offers wheelchair access or handy storage space.

bath faucets & tub fillers

These hardworking fixtures need to look great, operate smoothly, and stand up to daily abuse. Pay attention to both construction and style when choosing a faucet for your bath.

Faucet styles range from ornate Victorian designs to taps with modern, streamlined looks. Cross-shape handles offer vintage charm, while large wing levers add contemporary appeal. Two-handle models let you adjust water temperature more precisely with independent hot and cold controls, while single-handle models show off a sleek and contemporary aesthetic.

Faucet Styles

1. WIDESPREAD These faucets have a separate spout and handles spaced at least 8 inches apart.

2. CENTER-SET This compact style (water lines 4 inches apart) combines the spout and handles in one unit that mounts on the sink or countertop.

3. SINGLE-HANDLE Only one hole pierces the sink deck or countertop, saving space and allowing easy cleanup. A top- or side-mount lever or knob controls flow and temperature.

4. BRIDGE This nostalgic style's exposed channel links spoke-style handles and a curvy spout.

5. WALL-MOUNT Plumbed through the wall behind the sink, this type must be installed at the proper height to minimize splashing.

5. TUB FILLERS A deck-mount or Roman tub filler is a larger version of a sink faucet. Floor-mount tub fillers enhance freestanding tubs; waterfall fixtures add luxury.

MONEY-WISE

If your budget is limited, opt for a chrome finish. And keep in mind that two-handle faucets tend to be less expensive than single-handle faucets. But don't skimp on quality—paying more for solid-brass construction is worth it in the long run.

bathtubs

Thanks to smart materials and a variety of installation options, it's easy to create a soothing spot for soaking in any bathroom. Look for a tub that feels comfortable and suits your design style.

Tub Materials

Different tub materials offer perks that fit various price points and lifestyles. Take a look at the options and determine what will work best for you. Keep in mind, however, that not all tubs are available in all materials.

Cast-iron tubs are among the most durable and long-lasting fixtures in the home, and they can be refinished if needed. But these tubs are very heavy—even a small cast-iron tub will likely require extra floor support.

Acrylic has a high-gloss look that's similar to enameled cast iron but weighs much less. Acrylic is more durable and less prone to color-fade than fiberglass tubs. Repairs are much easier than those that must be made to porcelain surfaces.

Fiberglass tubs, also referred to as gel-coat fiberglass or fiberglass-reinforced plastic (FRP), feature a glossy, easy-to-clean surface. It's not as expensive as acrylic, but it's also not as durable and can crack if something hits it hard enough.

Composite tubs are made from an engineered material coated in enamel. They offer the heat-retention of a cast-iron tub at a third of the weight—so they are ideal candidates for upper-level bathrooms.

Cultured marble is a solid-surfacing material comparable to quartz-surfacing countertops that is produced from crushed marble set in resin and then covered with a clear gelcoat. Scratches can be buffed out of this material, but cracks can't be repaired.

Porcelain-on-steel tubs offer the look and heat-retention of cast iron at a lighter weight. Prices can vary, but keep in mind that you generally get what you pay for; lower-price models tend to chip and sound echoey.

Installation Methods

Select an installation method that works best with your space requirements to transform your tub into a stunning focal point.

Alcove: Commonly referred to as a recessed tub, this installation is used for rectangular tubs adjacent to three walls. The most common and affordable configuration, it features only one finished side and is often paired with wall-mount fixtures. If you're replacing a standard tub, take note of the drain location as you face the accessible side—this is how you determine if you need a left-hand or right-hand installation to match up with existing plumbing lines.

Platform: Tubs made for platform installation drop into a deck structure usually built into its own enclosure, often adjacent to the shower. This method works well with whirlpools and air baths, because space below the deck can house and hide pumps, plumbing, and hardware. (Keep these parts accessible with a removable panel.)

Undermount: The difference between a platform tub and an undermount tub, *above,* is mostly a matter of aesthetics. An undermount's rim is covered with a deck top—usually stone or tile that coordinates with surrounding materials—and it's supported from underneath, rather than

hanging from the deck as a platform tub does. Undermount tubs are often more expensive to install than platform models, but they make getting in and out of the tub easier.

Freestanding: As the name implies, this tub stands on its own on the bathroom floor without additional support, creating a stunning focal point. Tubs include classic claw-foot models, *opposite,* as well as streamlined, contemporary versions. This type of installation must be placed close to plumbing lines, so ask your design professional if this is an option in your space.

showerheads & enclosures

Combine multiple showerheads and body sprays to create a spa-like retreat. Whether you install a combination tub/shower unit or splurge on a separate shower, it's easy to include luxurious features.

Showerhead Options

The easiest and least expensive shower upgrade is switching out a standard showerhead with a model that offers a range of massaging spray patterns. When shopping, look for WaterSense-labeled products that use no more than 2.0 gallons of water per minute (rather than the standard 2.5 gpm). To ensure good performance with less water, look for new models that infuse air with the water to create a more voluminous spray. Also consider adding a handheld showerhead to the mix; models that slide up and down on a bar mounted to the wall can be ideal for a shower that will be used by people of varying heights. For added luxury, consider installing a ceiling-mount fixture, such as an oversize rain-style showerhead.

Body Sprays

If your shower space is large enough, or you're planning plumbing lines in adjacent walls, consider splurging on massaging body sprays that can enhance and customize your showering experience. Be sure to consult a plumber to determine how much work is involved and whether your home's water pressure can adequately supply the shower's expanded spray system.

Digital Controls

For the ultimate convenience, consider installing one of the new digital showering systems. These systems allow you to set preferences for water temperature, spray modes, steam, music, and more—for multiple users. They also help save water, because they will shut off the water and hold that temperature until you get in—or turn off the water after a set amount of time.

Shower Enclosures and Doors

Enclosures range from compact corner units to spacious shower rooms. Some prefabricated surrounds are sold as kits, which are easy to bring home and assemble inside your bathroom. Glass or translucent plastic doors help a shower feel big and bright, *left.* Choose sliding doors for tub/shower combos, swinging doors for freestanding units, and bifold or neo-angle doors for corner enclosures. Hinged shower shields partially screen a shower opening. Nearby flooring should be able to take a bit of spray.

DIY TIP

Don't want to hire a plumber to upgrade your shower? Look for easy-to-install preplumbed shower panels. These systems include multiple showerheads and body sprays in one compact unit. They can be easily retrofitted into most existing showers.

toilets

New designs conserve water, enhance comfort, and ease cleaning tasks. Take time to research flushing systems and compare design styles before deciding on a model.

Efficient Performance

New technology allows toilets to use less water without sacrificing performance. Today, the standard toilet uses 1.6 gallons per flush rather than the 3–7 gallons used by older models—and some new models offer even greater water savings. Because toilets account for nearly 30 percent of residential water usage, purchasing an efficient toilet can greatly decrease your home's water usage.

High-efficiency toilets employ powerful flushing systems and use 1.28 gallons or less per flush, instead of the standard 1.6 gallons. Dual-flush models let you select a partial flush for liquid waste or a full flush for solid waste. When shopping for a new toilet, look for a WaterSense-labeled product that has been tested to ensure both high efficiency and strong performance.

Toilet Design

Comfort-height models stand at chair height, making it easier to get up and down. You'll also need to decide if you want one-piece or two-piece construction. One-piece designs are easier to clean because they don't have a seam between the tank and the bowl—but they are typically more expensive.

MONEY-WISE

Bidets offer a cleansing spray of water, as well as luxurious features such as adjustable water temperature and heated seats. If you want this top-of-the-line technology at a more affordable price, look for bidet seats that can be attached to existing toilet seats.

Smart Features

NEW DESIGNS BOOST PERFORMANCE AND ENHANCE COMFORT.

Quieter operation. Gravity-feed models are usually quieter (and easier to maintain) than pressure-assisted flushing systems.

Elongated bowls. These toilets offer greater comfort—although round bowls take up less space, so they may be better for small baths.

Wider flapper valves and larger trapways. Look for these features to decrease the potential for clogging.

Quiet-close hinges. These ensure the toilet seat never slams.

Transitional toilet seats. Designed for young children, these seats are integrated into some standard toilet seats, eliminating the need to take potty-training seats on and off the family toilet.

Sleek designs. Concealed trapways and one-piece construction ease cleaning tasks.

bathroom lighting

Make your bathroom shine with a lighting plan that beautifully illuminates grooming areas and sets the mood for relaxation. Here's what to know before purchasing light fixtures.

In recent years bathrooms have become more than just utilitarian spaces. Now they are luxurious rooms for recharging and relaxing. As such, they need an efficient lighting plan that includes task lighting in targeted areas and overall lighting to set a sophisticated mood. Here are the most important components of a good lighting plan.

Task Lighting
Plan to include hardworking task lighting at the vanities, where grooming is done. Instead of installing recessed ceiling fixtures that cast shadows on the face, opt for vertical fixtures or sconces on either side of the mirror. If space doesn't allow lighting on both sides of the mirror, you can mount lights directly to the mirror (expect a higher cost) or opt for strip lighting above the mirror that evenly distributes light over the hair and face.

Also plan to include task lighting in the shower and tub areas; the light should be bright enough to ease cleaning and shaving tasks (and allow you to read shampoo labels). Select recessed downlights designed for use in wet areas, such as the shower and tub. If you plan to read in the tub, consider including an adjustable accent light aimed at the tub. If you'll have a separate toilet compartment, plan to include a single recessed downlight or surface fixture in this area as well.

Ambient Lighting
This type of lighting provides general illumination for the room and substitutes for natural lighting when it's not available.

Commonly, a surface-mount ceiling light is used in the center of the room, but a pendant light or chandelier can provide mood lighting and additional drama. You can also add a gentle glow around the perimeter of the room with cove lighting. In this scenario, rope lights are hidden behind a molding installed several inches below the ceiling.

Accent Lighting
If you plan to include a favorite piece of artwork or other cherished object in your bath, consider highlighting it with a small recessed spotlight. This technique can also bring extra attention to an above-counter sink or beautiful tilework.

DIY TIP
To properly illuminate your face, place your vanity lights about 60 inches from the floor—so the bottom of the shades are about eye level.

bathroom ventilation

Remove moisture and odors with hardworking ventilation fans that help keep your bathroom looking great. Today's models seamlessly pair updated style and function.

Bath fans are especially important in today's airtight homes. They help keep indoor moisture levels down, prevent the growth of mold and mildew, and put an end to foggy mirrors and peeling paint and wallpaper. It's best to vent the exhaust outside your home, rather than between floor joists or to an unheated attic, where the extra humidity can lead to mold that damages floors, walls, and ceiling materials.

Airflow Capacity

When you shop for a new ventilation fan, you'll see they feature different airflow capacities, measured in cubic feet per minute (cfm). The Home Ventilating Institute recommends that fans should have an airflow of 1 cfm for every square foot of bathroom space. For bathrooms larger than 100 square feet, you'll need to add 50 cfm for each toilet, shower, and bathtub, and 100 cfm for a whirlpool tub.

Noise Level

The noise level for bath fans is measured in sones. Fans that rate 0.5–1.2 sones are extremely quiet, while fans with ratings of 4.0 or more are quite noisy.

Energy Efficiency

As you're shopping, look for Energy Star models that use about 60 percent less energy than standard fans. Many of today's quieter motors also improve energy efficiency.

Smart Features

LOOK FOR OPTIONS THAT INCREASE CONVENIENCE.

Fan/light combination. Featuring a fan and light in one unit, these models can use existing wiring for a ceiling light; many feature stylish designs and decorative finishes.

Built-in heater. Fan-forced heat or infrared radiant bulbs warm the bathroom on chilly days.

Sensors. Models with motion sensors turn on automatically when someone enters the room. Other models turn on and off based on humidity levels in the bathroom.

Heat exchanger. These pricey models use warm, outgoing air to heat cooler, incoming air—reducing heat loss.

wish list

Use these checklists to help you determine what elements you need and want in your kitchen or bath. Then devise a smart remodeling plan that will keep your project on track.

kitchens

baths

kitchen wish list

Before beginning construction work, take time to consider your overall goals, devise an efficient layout for your kitchen work zone, and determine a budget for your project.

Whether you'll be hiring a pro for your kitchen renovation or doing the work yourself, this handy checklist can help you keep track of all the details. Answer as many questions as you can before meeting with a designer or architect, then take this checklist with you. Thinking about your needs and goals in advance can help you make the best use of your meeting time and set up your remodeling project for success.

Determine Your Needs

Take time to think about what works in your current kitchen—and what doesn't—to help you design a space that suits your lifestyle.

What do you love about your current kitchen?

_____

_____

What would you most like to change?

_____

_____

Describe your dream kitchen:

_____

_____

What type of feeling would you like your new kitchen to have?

_____

_____

What colors do you like?

_____

_____

How do you describe your decorating style?

_____

_____

Do you want to include multiple workstations?

_____

_____

Do you want your kitchen to be open to the family room or other living spaces?

_____

_____

Number and age of household members:

_____

_____

Number and age of cooks:

_____

_____

Does anyone using the kitchen have any physical limitations? Please explain.

_____

_____

How many times per month do you entertain?

_____

Do you host large events or small gatherings?

_____

How long do you intend to live in your current home?

_____

Kitchen Activities and Storage

Determine what activities you'll do in your kitchen and where these activities will take place. Take an inventory of everything you want to store in your new space, and consider where these items will be used.

Cooking

	YES	NO
Light cooking (fast meals, easy preparation)	☐	☐
Family cooking (large meals, partially from scratch)	☐	☐
Gourmet cooking	☐	☐
Baking	☐	☐
Entertaining (serving outside the kitchen)	☐	☐
Cooking parties as entertaining	☐	☐

Dining

	YES	NO
Informal dining for fewer than six	☐	☐
Informal dining for six or more	☐	☐
Formal dining	☐	☐

Other Kitchen Activites

	YES	NO
Office/computer work	☐	☐
Crafts	☐	☐
Sewing	☐	☐
Homework	☐	☐
Games	☐	☐
TV viewing (in kitchen or from kitchen area)	☐	☐
Laundry: machine-wash, hand-wash, air-dry, sort/fold	☐	☐
Talking on the phone	☐	☐
Listening to music	☐	☐
Displaying collections	☐	☐
Growing herbs/plants	☐	☐

Storage by Item Type

Food/Beverages

	YES	NO
Staples, canned goods	☐	☐
Fruits, vegetables	☐	☐
Spices, oils, vinegars	☐	☐
Coffee, espresso, tea	☐	☐
Wine	☐	☐
Other:_____		

Cookware

	YES	NO
Bakeware	☐	☐
Pots and pans	☐	☐
Measuring cups, spoons	☐	☐
Specialty utensils, such as funnels	☐	☐
Cookbooks, recipes	☐	☐
Small appliances	☐	☐
Other:_____		

Dishes/Serving

	YES	NO
Everyday dinnerware, glassware	☐	☐
Table linens, napkins	☐	☐
Special-occasion dinnerware, glassware	☐	☐
Flatware	☐	☐
Serving pieces (platters, tureens, pitchers)	☐	☐
Other:_____		

Other

	YES	NO
Paper goods	☐	☐
Food storage containers/wraps	☐	☐
Pet food and supplies	☐	☐
Cleaning products	☐	☐

Storage Accessories

Base Cabinets

	YES	NO
Full-extension sliding shelves	☐	☐
Hinged swing-out wire shelf units (for blind corners)	☐	☐
Lazy Susan systems (for corner cabinets)	☐	☐
Door-mount racks for food pantry	☐	☐
Slide-out racks/bins for trash and recycling	☐	☐
Dedicated racks for pots and pans, with lid dividers	☐	☐
Controlled-close drawer systems	☐	☐
Deep drawers with pegs	☐	☐

Wall Cabinets

	YES	NO
Pull-down overhead shelf systems	☐	☐
Flip-down cookbook shelf, mounted to underside	☐	☐

Miscellaneous

	YES	NO
Backsplash rack system for utensils and spices	☐	☐
Ceiling-mount pot rack	☐	☐
Cabinet for TV	☐	☐
Other:_____		

kitchen wish list

Physical Properties

Now that you've thought about how you'll use your new kitchen, consider its physical properties. Go through the following checklists and think about the elements you want to change and/or include. Your designer can help you assess what elements will fit into your space.

Room Size

	Existing Kitchen	New Kitchen
North wall	_____	_____
East wall	_____	_____
South wall	_____	_____
West wall	_____	_____
Total square feet	_____	_____
Ceiling height	_____	_____

Cabinets

Style:
- ☐ Traditional
- ☐ Contemporary
- ☐ Transitional
- ☐ Cottage
- ☐ Period look (specify)_____

Door surface:
- ☐ Wood   Species _____ Finish _____
- ☐ Laminate or vinyl thermal overlay
- ☐ Metal

Door style:
Full overlay _____ Partial overlay_____ Inset _____

	YES	NO
Multiple finishes	☐	☐
Cabinet hardware	☐	☐
Island	☐	☐
Matching range hood	☐	☐
Matching appliance panels	☐	☐

Surfaces

	Backsplash	Countertop
Ceramic tile	☐	☐
Concrete	☐	☐
Laminate	☐	☐
Quartz-surfacing (engineered stone)	☐	☐
Solid-surfacing	☐	☐
Stainless steel	☐	☐
Stone	☐	☐
Wood	☐	☐

Other:_____

Flooring

Flooring	YES	NO	Where?
Bamboo	☐	☐	_____
Carpet	☐	☐	_____
Ceramic tile	☐	☐	_____
Concrete	☐	☐	_____
Cork	☐	☐	_____
Laminate	☐	☐	_____
Linoleum	☐	☐	_____
Porcelain tile	☐	☐	_____
Vinyl sheet	☐	☐	_____
Vinyl tile	☐	☐	_____
Wood (solid)	☐	☐	_____
Wood (engineered)	☐	☐	_____
Stone	☐	☐	_____

Other:_____

Sink 1

Material:
- ☐ Acrylic
- ☐ Cast iron
- ☐ Composite
- ☐ Enameled steel
- ☐ Solid-surfacing
- ☐ Stainless steel
- ☐ Stone

Configuration:
- ☐ Single-basin
- ☐ Double-basin
- ☐ Triple-basin
- ☐ Apron-front
- ☐ Prep sink

Other:_____

Fixtures:
- ☐ Single-handle faucet
- ☐ Bridge faucet
- ☐ High-arc faucet
- ☐ Pullout faucet
- ☐ Pot-filler faucet
- ☐ Wall-mount faucet
- ☐ Built-in water filter
- ☐ Built-in soap/lotion dispenser
- ☐ Food waste disposer

Sink 2

Material:
- ☐ Acrylic
- ☐ Cast iron
- ☐ Composite
- ☐ Enameled steel
- ☐ Solid-surfacing
- ☐ Stainless steel
- ☐ Stone

Configuration:
- ☐ Single-basin
- ☐ Double-basin
- ☐ Triple-basin
- ☐ Apron-front
- ☐ Prep sink

Other:_____

Fixtures:
- ☐ Single-handle faucet
- ☐ Bridge faucet
- ☐ High-arc faucet
- ☐ Pullout faucet
- ☐ Pot-filler faucet
- ☐ Wall-mount faucet
- ☐ Built-in water filter
- ☐ Built-in soap/lotion dispenser
- ☐ Food waste disposer

Ventilation and Lighting

	YES	NO
Chimney hood	☐	☐
Custom insert	☐	☐
Downdraft	☐	☐
Island hood	☐	☐
Microwave/hood combination	☐	☐
Undercabinet hood	☐	☐
Pendant lights	☐	☐
Recessed lighting	☐	☐
Skylight	☐	☐
Task lighting	☐	☐
Accent lighting	☐	☐

Other: _____

_____

Large Appliances

☐ Conventional oven   Qty: _____
☐ Convection oven   Qty: _____
☐ Microwave oven   Qty: _____
☐ Steam oven
☐ Cooktop
☐ Freestanding range
☐ Slide-in range
☐ Warming drawer
☐ Refrigerator   Qty: _____
☐ Freezer   Qty: _____
☐ Refrigerator drawer   Qty: _____
☐ Wine cooler
☐ Under-counter refrigerator
☐ Dishwasher   Qty: _____
☐ Dishwasher drawers   Qty: _____
☐ Clothes washer
☐ Clothes dryer
☐ Washer-dryer combination

Small Appliances

☐ Blender
☐ Bread machine
☐ Coffee grinder
☐ Coffeemaker
☐ Electric frying pan
☐ Electric griddle
☐ Electric toaster
☐ Electric wok
☐ Espresso/cappuccino machine
☐ Food dehydrator
☐ Food processor
☐ Hand mixer
☐ Ice cream/sorbet maker
☐ Indoor grill
☐ Juicer
☐ Pasta machine
☐ Popcorn popper
☐ Rice cooker
☐ Slow cooker
☐ Stand mixer
☐ Toaster
☐ Toaster oven

Money Management

Set up a budget for your remodeling project before any work begins, and take time to carefully consider how best to pay for the work.

Budget Planning

I plan to hire a contractor for all the work.	☐ Yes	☐ No
I plan to do some of the work myself.	☐ Yes	☐ No
I plan to do the decor, paint, etc. myself.	☐ Yes	☐ No
I plan to do all the work at once.	☐ Yes	☐ No
I plan to do the work and replace items in stages.	☐ Yes	☐ No

This is the realistic total I hope to spend: $ _____

This is the absolute most I can spend: $ _____

Financing Method

☐ All cash/savings $_____
☐ Home-equity loan/line of credit $_____
☐ Pay cash _____%, Borrow _____%

Notes

_____

_____

_____

bath wish list

Before beginning construction work, take time to consider your overall goals, devise an efficient layout for your bathroom, and determine a budget for your project.

Whether you'll be hiring a pro for your bathroom renovation or doing the work yourself, this handy checklist can help you keep track of all the details. Answer as many questions as you can before meeting with a designer or architect, then take this checklist with you. Thinking about your needs and goals in advance can help you make the best use of your meeting time and set up your remodeling project for success.

Determine Your Needs

Take time to think about what works in your current bathroom—and what doesn't—to help you design a space that suits your lifestyle.

What do you love about your current bath?

_____

_____

What would you most like to change?

_____

_____

Describe your dream bath:

_____

_____

What type of feeling would you like your new bathroom space to have?

_____

_____

What colors do you like?

_____

_____

Will more than one person be using the bathroom at the same time? How often?

_____

_____

What bathroom activities are better done in private?

_____

_____

What bathroom activities can be done in a shared space?

_____

_____

Will this bathroom be used by visitors? How often?

_____

_____

Will visitors be children, adults, or both?

_____

_____

Do any users have physical limitations?

_____

_____

Do you prefer separate showering and bathing areas?

_____

_____

Would you like a tub that accommodates more than one person?

_____

_____

Would you like a shower that accommodates more than one person?

_____

_____

Would you like a toilet and/or bidet placed in its own compartment?

_____

_____

To print this checklist, go to
BHG.com/KBGuide

Bath Activities and Storage

Determine what activities you'll do in your bathroom and where these activities will take place. Take an inventory of everything you'll need to store in your bath, and consider where these items will be used.

Grooming	YES	NO	Where?
			(i.e.: vanity, tub, shower)
Washing	☐	☐	_____
Shaving	☐	☐	_____
Brushing teeth/flossing	☐	☐	_____
Trimming/painting nails	☐	☐	_____
Applying cosmetics	☐	☐	_____
Drying/styling hair	☐	☐	_____
Skin care	☐	☐	_____
Taking medicines/vitamins	☐	☐	_____
Applying lotion	☐	☐	_____
First aid	☐	☐	_____

Showering and Bathing	YES	NO	Where?
			(i.e.: vanity, tub, shower)
Washing body	☐	☐	_____
Washing hair	☐	☐	_____
Soaking	☐	☐	_____
Bathing pets	☐	☐	_____
Assisting an adult with bathing	☐	☐	_____
Assisting a child with bathing	☐	☐	_____

Other Bath Activities	YES	NO	Where?
Personal pampering	☐	☐	_____
Undressing/hamper	☐	☐	_____
Dressing: clothes	☐	☐	_____
Dressing: underwear/sleep clothes	☐	☐	_____
Drinking beverages	☐	☐	_____
Eating snacks	☐	☐	_____
Exercise without equipment	☐	☐	_____
Exercise using equipment	☐	☐	_____
Laundry: air-dry	☐	☐	_____
Laundry: hand-wash	☐	☐	_____
Laundry: machine-wash	☐	☐	_____
Laundry: sort/fold	☐	☐	_____
Listening to music	☐	☐	_____
Massage	☐	☐	_____
Meditation	☐	☐	_____

Other Bath Activities *continued*	YES	NO	Where?
Polishing shoes	☐	☐	_____
Reading	☐	☐	_____
Supervising children	☐	☐	_____
Talking on the phone	☐	☐	_____
Tanning/sunning	☐	☐	_____
Watching television	☐	☐	_____
Displaying collections	☐	☐	_____
Growing plants	☐	☐	_____
Other:			_____

Storage and Space Planning

Storage by Item Type	YES	NO
Makeup	☐	☐
Shaving supplies	☐	☐
Hair grooming equipment/supplies	☐	☐
Hand/foot grooming equipment/supplies	☐	☐
Personal hygiene items	☐	☐
Medicine/first aid	☐	☐
Bathroom paper products	☐	☐
Bath towels and washcloths	☐	☐
Household bedroom linens	☐	☐
Exercise equipment	☐	☐
Pet grooming/bath supplies	☐	☐
Cleaning supplies	☐	☐
Shoe polishing supplies	☐	☐
Other:		

Extra Amenities	YES	NO
Blow dryer	☐	☐
Curling iron	☐	☐
Electric toothbrush	☐	☐
Electric razor	☐	☐
Fireplace	☐	☐
Radio/music player	☐	☐
Scale	☐	☐
Television/DVD player	☐	☐
Towel warmer	☐	☐
Coffeemaker	☐	☐
Mini fridge	☐	☐
Clothes washer/dryer	☐	☐
Other:		

bath wish list

Physical Properties

Now that you've thought about how you'll use your new bath, consider its physical properties. Go through the following checklists, and think about the elements you want to change and/or include. Your designer can help you assess what elements will fit into your space.

Room Size	Existing Bath	New Bath
North wall	_____	_____
East wall	_____	_____
South wall	_____	_____
West wall	_____	_____
Total square feet	_____	_____
Ceiling height	_____	_____

Flooring	Yes	No	Where?
Bamboo	☐	☐	_____
Ceramic tile	☐	☐	_____
Concrete	☐	☐	_____
Cork	☐	☐	_____
Laminate	☐	☐	_____
Linoleum	☐	☐	_____
Vinyl sheet	☐	☐	_____
Vinyl tile	☐	☐	_____
Wood (solid)	☐	☐	_____
Wood (engineered)	☐	☐	_____
Stone	☐	☐	_____

Other:_____

Toilet

☐ 1-piece low-profile
☐ 2-piece standard-height
☐ 2-piece comfort-height
☐ Wall-hung
☐ Round seat
☐ Elongated seat
☐ High-efficiency model
☐ Bidet

Other:_____

Shower

Shower wall material: _____
Shower floor/pan material: _____
Shower door material: _____

Showerhead: Type_____ Finish_____
Body spray:	☐ Yes	☐ No	Finish_____
Handheld shower:	☐ Yes	☐ No	Finish_____
Bench seat:	☐ Yes	☐ No	Material_____
Steam:	☐ Yes	☐ No	
Sauna:	☐ Yes	☐ No	
Accessible/curbless:	☐ Yes	☐ No	

Surfaces	Vanity	Shower Walls	Tub	Walls
Laminate	☐	☐	☐	☐
Solid-surfacing	☐	☐	☐	☐
Quartz (engineered stone)	☐	☐	☐	☐
Granite	☐	☐	☐	☐
Marble	☐	☐	☐	☐
Cultured marble	☐	☐	☐	☐
Tile (ceramic, porcelain, glass)	☐	☐	☐	☐
Wood	☐	☐	☐	☐
Concrete	☐	☐	☐	☐

Bathtub

Material:
☐ Cast iron
☐ Fiberglass
☐ Cultured marble
☐ Steel
☐ Acrylic
☐ Copper
☐ Stone

Other:_____

Configuration:
☐ Platform
☐ Skirted
☐ Platform with steps
☐ Freestanding

Fixtures:
Tub filler faucet:
☐ Deck-mount
☐ Wall-mount
☐ Floor-mount
Finish _____
Hand-held sprayer: ☐ Yes ☐ No Finish_____

Special Features:
Jetted:	☐ Yes	☐ No
Soaking tub:	☐ Yes	☐ No

Vanity

Style:
- ☐ Contemporary
- ☐ Transitional
- ☐ Traditional
- ☐ Cottage
- ☐ Period look (specify) _____

Door surface:
- ☐ Wood   Species_____Finish_____
- ☐ Laminate or vinyl thermal overlay_____

Multiple surfaces:	☐ Yes	☐ No	
Cabinet hardware:	☐ Yes	☐ No	
Medicine cabinet(s):	☐ Yes	☐ No	
Defogging mirror:	☐ Yes	☐ No	

Other:_____
_____

Lavatory/Sink

Material:
- ☐ Porcelain
- ☐ Glass
- ☐ Cast iron
- ☐ Stainless steel
- ☐ Decorative metal
- ☐ Composite
- ☐ Stone

Configuration:
- ☐ Pedestal
- ☐ Top-mount
- ☐ Undermount
- ☐ Wall-hung
- ☐ Vessel
- ☐ Integral/seamless

Other:_____
_____

Fixtures:
- ☐ Deck-mount 4-inch center; Finish_____
- ☐ Deck-mount 8-inch center; Finish_____
- ☐ Deck-mount single-hole; Finish_____
- ☐ Wall-mount; Finish_____

Other:_____
_____

Accessories

Glass shelves	Qty_____	Finish_____
Medicine cabinet	Qty_____	Finish_____
Mirror	Qty_____	Finish_____
Towel bars	Qty_____	Finish_____
Towel rings	Qty_____	Finish_____
Robe hooks	Qty_____	Finish_____
Shower grab bars	Qty_____	Finish_____
Tub grab bars	Qty_____	Finish_____
Toilet grab bars	Qty_____	Finish_____
Toilet paper holder	Qty_____	Finish_____
Television	Qty_____	Finish_____

Ventilation and Lighting

	Yes	No
Fan	☐	☐
Fan/light combination	☐	☐
Fan/light/heat combination	☐	☐
Ambient (general) lighting	☐	☐
Skylight	☐	☐
Task lighting (vanity/dressing table)	☐	☐
Accent (decorative) lighting	☐	☐

Other:_____
_____

Money Management

Set up a budget for your remodeling project before any work begins, and take time to carefully consider how best to pay for the work.

Budget Planning

	Yes	No
I plan to hire a contractor for all the work.	☐ Yes	☐ No
I plan to do some of the work myself.	☐ Yes	☐ No
I plan to do the decor, paint, etc. myself.	☐ Yes	☐ No
I plan to do all the work at once.	☐ Yes	☐ No
I plan to do the work and replace items in stages.	☐ Yes	☐ No

This is the realistic total I hope to spend: $ _____
This is the absolute most I can spend: $ _____

Financing Method
- ☐ All cash/savings $_____
- ☐ Home-equity loan/line of credit $_____
- ☐ Pay cash _____%, Borrow _____%

Notes
_____
_____
_____

Index

Index

live with *stule*

Look for budget-friendly home improvements, smart decoratir and space-saving solutions in th Better Homes and Gardens° boc

Better Homes and Gardens.

△▽○

An Imprint of HMH

NEW DECORATING BOOK

Better Homes and Gardens.
small bath solutions

COLOR
the complete guide for your home

• Paints
• Palettes
• Patterns

room-by-room solutions
makeovers

before

ORGANIZE
your home
CLUTTER CURES
for EVERY ROOM

New
Cottage Style